STAY OR LEAVE

- resume writing
  workshop on wenzelor

- civil service test
  also jobs that don't
  require test

Also by Barry and Linda Gale
Discover What You're Best At

STAY OR LEAVE

BARRY AND LINDA GALE

PERENNIAL LIBRARY

Harper & Row, Publishers, New York
Grand Rapids, Philadelphia, St. Louis, San Francisco
London, Singapore, Sydney, Tokyo

Stay or Leave is based on an idea of Reid Boates.

FIRST EDITION

Designed by Abigail Sturges

LIBRARY OF CONGRESS CATALOGING-IN-PUBLICATION DATA

Gale, Barry.
    Stay or leave / Barry and Linda Gale. — 1st ed.
      p.   cm.
    ISBN 0-06-096278-X (pbk.)
     1. Career changes—Decision making. 2. Career changes—
   Case studies. I. Gale, Linda. II. Title.
HF5384.G35 1989
650'.4—dc20   88-45932

89 90 91 92 93 WG/RRD 10 9 8 7 6 5 4 3 2 1

In memory of Dad—
you were the best

Contents

Part 1: The Stay or Leave Decision-making System   **11**

It's for You   13
Why Might You Change Jobs?   13
The Seven Warning Signals   14
Jobs by Accident   14
Decide to Decide   14
How Will You Benefit from *Stay or Leave?*   15
How Does It Work?   15
About the Test   16
Some Important Words of Caution   17

Part 2: The Tests   **19**

Relationships/Office Politics Test   21
Decide if you're comfortable in your company culture. Is being a
"team player" for you? Do you and your boss get along? Does your
supervisor relate to your needs and recognize your potential, or does
he or she turn good people like you into deadwood? Do your
relationships with coworkers suggest you stay, look around or leave?
Can you recognize politically charged situations and deal with them
effectively? Simply put: Do you fit in?

Values/Skills Test   39
It's time to rank your values in order of their priority to you and
evaluate your current level of job satisfaction. Has time changed your
on-the-job values? Evaluate your growth and determine how much
further you can go. Have you reached the peak in your job? Is it time
to transfer? Decide how your experiences and accomplishments have
enhanced your skills. Evaluate your immediate, midterm and long-
range goals. Would a different job fulfill your goals faster? Are you
having a state-of-the-art experience?

Company/Rewards Test   63
Is your company growing, stagnating or dying? Is it concerned about
your growth? Is your industry becoming obsolete? Are you in sync
with your company culture? Have you mastered the art of delegation
and are you now ready to move up? Which rewards of success are for
you . . . salary, perks, power, travel, status, freedom to experiment, a
sense of accomplishment? Are they available where you are employed?

Stress Test   81

Are you experiencing today's common workplace illness? If so, which
types of stress affect you? Do you manifest the symptoms of
indecision? Do you imagine everything to be far worse than it actually
is? How often do you take home your office problems in your
attache? Determine if your stresses motivate you or are self-
destructive. Do they contaminate the quality of your personal life?

Entrepreneurship Test   91

Do you have what it takes to turn a potential dream into a going
venture? Are your work-related self-concept and temperament in tune
with entrepreneurship? Are you willing to take risks and accept the
responsibilities entrepreneuring requires? Could you go the next six
months without a salary? Which are you . . . a strategist, a planner or
a doer?

Job-changing Test   99

Are you ready to leave your job? What inconveniences might you
encounter and how would you react to them? What personal reasons
could prevent you from relocating? Are you caught up in the "grass-
is-greener" syndrome, thinking any other job must be better than
your present one? Are you ready to leave your friends, benefits and
seniority behind? Is there an alarm clock ticking in your head, saying,
"It's time to change"?

Part 3: Scoring   **111**

Scoring Your Tests   113
Scoring Keys and Tally Sheets   114

Part 4: What Your Scores Reveal   **133**

Your Personal Profile   135
Possible Personal Profiles   136
Prescriptions   137

Part 5: Answer Sheets   **139**

About the People Interviewed   **149**

Acknowledgments   159

Stories of Real-Life Stay or Leave Decisions

Paul H. Alvarez	87
Dr. Joyce Brothers	65
J. Carter Brown	101
Art Buchwald	42
Charlie Byrd	46
Alan Cranston	48
Gary Edwards	66
Eileen Ford	22
Joe Franklin	68
Doug Fraser	104
Tom Freston	50
Mary Futrell	106
Kevin C. Gottlieb	26
Robert Gray	70
Peter D. Hart	71
Judith Richards Hope	74
Larry King	54
Knight Kiplinger	107
Gabe Mirkin, M.D.	92
Rose Narva	108
Jerome Navies	94
Mike Nevard	76
Ike Pappas	56
Patrick Roddy	28
Stephen I. Schlossberg	78
Paul Sorvino	58
Paul Steinle	96
Preston Robert Tisch	109
Jack Valenti	88
Caspar Willard Weinberger	96
Eddie R. White	110
George F. Will	59
Bob Woodward	30
V. Orville Wright	36
Duke Zeibert	97

PART 1

THE STAY OR LEAVE DECISION-MAKING SYSTEM

It's for You

Let's assume you're good at what you do and you're concerned about your future.

Honestly now, when was the last time you asked yourself whether you should stay with your present company/organization in your present position or start to think about moving elsewhere?

We'll bet the answer is something along the lines of "An hour ago." Or "Last payday." Or "At least two or three times a year."

Your reasons can be entirely personal, entirely professional, or entirely mixed. And you are not alone. The Stay or Leave dilemma occurs with amazing frequency among most good workers. Our experience as career consultants indicates that if you're an above-average person, you will make the decision to change jobs eight times during the course of your career. However, the decision to change is often made on a wing and a prayer and with a dash or two of emotion.

And how many times will you *think* about changing jobs? The answer has to be dozens, if not hundreds. This book will alert you to the key issues to consider and give you a quantifiable system to follow each time you face the mind-boggling decision either to stay and improve your current job situation, or leave and pack your traveling bag. Simply put: *Stay or Leave* will help you think clearly, deeply and decisively about whether or not to leave your current position. It's a "*before* you decide to leave" book.

Why Might You Change Jobs?

Although there are many possible reasons, we have found that the majority of relatively high performers move to new positions because of:

- Limited personal growth opportunities
- Restrictions that inhibit their ability to do their best work
- Personality conflicts with superiors or coworkers
- Insufficient recognition or compensation
- Economic realignments, mergers and acquisitions.

Think about it. Does the reason for your last change fall into one of these categories?

The Seven Warning Signals

Not surprisingly, our research indicates that a "personality conflict" is the most frequently cited reason for leaving. Often this departure is involuntary and unexpected by the employee. That's right, unexpected by the terminated employee because, unwittingly, he or she ignored some of the seven warning signals that usually precede the pink slip. Have you experienced any of them lately?

1. You're bored silly. Your work no longer seems to challenge you. Each day feels like a carbon copy.
2. You no longer seem to be getting the interesting assignments. Others do.
3. You're way past due for a raise or promotion.
4. No one asks for your opinion anymore. It's as if you didn't exist.
5. Someone higher in the chain of command seems to be constantly finding fault with your work.
6. Your coworkers seem to be avoiding you.
7. Your boss won't look you in the eye.

If you nodded "yes" once or twice, it's time to get your act together and attempt to improve your current situation. If even more signals are there, you're living on borrowed time. However, the signals are not always easily understood. They may not be sent out clearly. That happens sometimes. More likely, the intended recipient misses the telltale signs. It's quite true . . . people hear only what they want to hear, see only what they want to see, and understand only what they want to understand. Well, this book will remedy that.

Jobs by Accident

Let's also bear in mind that five out of six of us find ourselves in our job or career by accident. That's right. Not by design or as the result of thorough career planning, but by accident. Think about your current job and perhaps the previous one or two that led you to this point in your career. Did you painstakingly plan it, or did you somehow stumble into it?

So it should come as no surprise to you that you may be among those who are in the wrong job: unchallenged, unappreciated, exploited and unhappy. If you're feeling this way, there is something you can do.

Decide to Decide

That's right, decide to decide. Sounds simple, doesn't it? However, this vital first step is often avoided because decision-making entails taking some risk. And too many people mistakenly equate risk-taking with probable failure. Well, that's just not true! We have found that people who avoid risks make only two or three major mistakes each year; and those who are prone to boldly take risks generally make two or three major mistakes a year. It's a tossup. So what do you do now?

We'll repeat: Decide to decide. You've nothing to lose and a lot to gain. For as you go through the decision-making process, you will gain a new perspective that will bring the right decision clearly into focus.

How Will You Benefit from Stay or Leave?

- You will use an objective, measurable way to dramatically increase your odds of making the right decision, rather than leaving the selection to luck, a whim, a fit of anger or what your best friend thinks you should do.
- You will reach one of three specific conclusions:
     You've got it pretty good after all, so for your own sake *stay*;
     Stay, but keep your eye on things and take the test again soon;
     Scary as the prospect might seem, *leave*.
- You will become aware of the intricacies hidden within the key issues you face as you pinpoint the areas of your discontent.
- You will objectively clarify your perception of your current situation and be able to make good use of this information as you evaluate possible future jobs.
- You will more fully appreciate that certain genuine, restless instinct you share with other high performers and understand why some wisely stay put.
- You will have the advantage of establishing a current benchmark, so that you can retake the test in a few months and determine if you've moved closer to a Stay or Leave decision.

Finally, both to inspire and to remind you that you're not alone, we have interspersed dozens of insights from real people, many quite well known, that we have drawn from the exclusive interviews we conducted during preparation of this book.

How Does It Work?

Stay or Leave is a professionally devised, self-administered and self-scored inventory of questions designed to help you discover, evaluate and measure the length, breadth and depth of your opportunities at your current job. The multifaceted tests will rate your perceptions of office politics, your relationships with your boss and coworkers, your goals and rewards, your potentials for growth, your present values and skills, your chances as an entrepreneur, the amount of stress you may be experiencing, the current state of your company and industry, job changing and much more.

After taking the tests you'll score yourself using the objective scoring system on pages 113–131. Armed with your scores and newly found insights you'll be better able to decide whether you're in the right place *for now*. And that's what you're trying to determine.

About the Test

Let's start with a few words about test anxiety. We know how much nervous tension the word "test" may have created when you were a youngster. Then, it seemed that your whole life depended upon finding the right answers to scholastic math tests, obtaining your driver's license and performing well on college entrance exams. But that's all in the past. Now, you're doing this for *yourself*. No one else is going to see your answers and no one is going to judge them. So, first of all, relax.

The format of the questions in this book varies. Some questions take a very simple form, such as "Select *a, b* or *c*," while others are more involved and require you to "assemble" a final answer from the information given.

There are no "right" or "wrong" answers. The questions are designed to tap your perceptions and put you in touch with your feelings as you examine your past experiences, current situation and future expectations. So, do not respond as you think some other people might want you to; respond the way you want to.

Each response is assigned *S*tay points or *L*eave points. The specific number of points attributed is proportionally weighted along a continuum that ranges from 5*S* (a strong stay signal . . . a great place to be!) to 1*S* (a mild stay signal . . . okay), and from 1*L* (a mild leave signal . . . yes, maybe slightly uncomfortable) to 5*L* (a strong leave signal . . . a disaster, get out!).

For example, consider two possible responses to a question about the relationship between employee and boss. "My boss is jealous of my abilities and constantly undermines and sabotages my progress." That's a critical situation and a strong reason to consider leaving. A score of 5*L* is appropriate. "My boss keeps silent and rarely compliments me for a job well done." Also a reason to leave, but a mild one. A score of 1*L* is appropriate. It's true, both answers are reasons to leave . . . but they are *unequally* important.

Most of the questions are straightforward and require only a second or two to answer, while some others are quite complex and will require considerably more time. Take whatever time you need; the tests have no time limits. With that in mind, you'll find certain questions may trigger memories and mental images of former events in your life. It's possible you could "wander down memory lane" for a moment or two. That's okay. We encourage you to do so, for it's a healthy form of introspection and a little daydreaming may even lead you to a clearer and deeper understanding of your current situation.

You should answer every question in the book. Even if you feel you do not have concerns in one of the six test areas, it's essential to get the total, overall picture before you can make your final decision to Stay or Leave.

Some Important Words of Caution

Before you begin the tests, three brief caveats.

1. Don't take any of the tests if you have just had a major argument with your boss, learned you've been denied a promotion, etc. You want to obtain an objective, rational view of your situation and that will be more likely to happen if you're in a more even-tempered mood.
2. Don't skip questions because the answer choices given do not exactly fit your situation. At times, you might feel that if you could construct an additional answer it would be a better response than those presented. This may be true. But your task is to select the answer that is best from those given.
3. Don't make it more difficult than it is. While you'll want to examine each question thoroughly before you respond, you should not turn questions inside-out looking for meanings that were never intended. That may lead to answers you never intended.

In addition, no test results should be taken as the absolute and indisputable solution to workplace problems. Tests are tools, not end-alls and these are no exception. So if your results indicate a strong leave signal, does that mean you should walk into work tomorrow and quit? Of course not. You'll need to tidy up your current situation and line up your next position before you hand in your resignation.

And if your results indicate a strong stay signal, does that mean you're destined to remain at your current job forever? Again, of course not. Economics change, industries change, bosses change, and your values and needs change. If and when those things happen, retake this test and you'll see that your scores have changed.

So, it all boils down to this: Don't expect a test to actually make decisions for you; all it can do is point you in the right direction. The rest is up to you.

Now, let's get started. Let's determine if you should Stay or Leave.

PART 2
THE TESTS

Relationships/Office Politics Test

1. Pilot and copilot, manager and assistant manager, and many married couples may tell you, "Two heads are better than one." From their perspective, they might be right. But if your job is structured in such a way that you report to two bosses, beware. If the two have frequent difficulties making decisions cooperatively, or if they do not get along personally, you might find yourself right in the middle of a battlefield that could negatively affect your career.

    Is your job structured so that you must report to two or more bosses?

    a. yes
    b. no

2. Of course, it isn't fair. But it's a fact and there's no escaping it. Office politics is a part of every organization and it creates a visible and invisible chain of power that can determine your fate. If you're aware of the power structures, you'll be more likely to survive and rise. Lack of awareness results in undue pressure and stagnation.

    Would you say you have a clear understanding of how far your immediate boss's power extends?

    a. yes
    b. no

3. Are you aware of fellow employees who are well connected to the upper-level decision-makers because they are relatives or former coworkers, or are romantically linked?

    a. yes
    b. no

4. How many of the following occur where you work?

    • Employees respond to the boss with exaggerated expressions such as "Yesss, Sirrr!"
    • Your boss exclaims, *"Even you* should be able to understand this!"
    • When employees talk with their boss they preface their remarks with comments such as "I'm sure you'll think this is a stupid idea, but maybe . . ."
    • Conversations stop when the supervisor suddenly enters the room.

    a. all four of the above
    b. three of the above
    c. two of the above
    d. one or none of the above

Eileen Ford went through a few jobs before becoming a copywriter and then a stylist. Her agency, the internationally renowned Ford Models, Inc., began with just two models and was conducted from her home. During Linda's visit to the Manhattan office of Ford Models, Ms. Ford told many stories of her career. It was obvious that when she works, she works, and when she plays, she plays as hard as she works. Eileen Ford is full of life, guts, and lots of fun. The following story is Linda's favorite:

"When I graduated from college, I worked for an air cargo company. And my job was to obtain ration coupons for gasoline, tires, whatever it was that was rationed. The personnel director told me we were owned by a steamship company and its director needed extra coupons for his wife. As far as I was concerned, he didn't need any coupons and certainly, above all, his wife didn't. My boss told me to get them. I thought about it and knew I was in deep trouble. This was my first job and I felt it was dishonest. I stood there wondering what to do. Here I was wearing a Brooks Brothers sweater, you know, long and baggy, the type that goes with saddle shoes. I was nervously twisting the bottom of it, not realizing I was tugging it down in the process . . . when my boss suddenly said 'Don't try to show your breasts to me.' I turned around and walked out. I got into my car and never came back."

5. When was the last time you were invited to lunch by employees ranking a step or two up the chain of command?

    a. within the past six months
    b. within the past year
    c. about two years ago
    d. "Are you kidding? I've never been asked."

6. I guess I can say I'm well-liked by almost everyone, not only in my own department but in others as well. When it's time for me to be a candidate for promotion, I should have many supporters.

    a. That's me, more or less.
    b. That's not really me.

7. What do you think would happen if (or what happened when) you went to your boss with a suggestion for changing the method of performing a rather routine job? She would (or did) . . .

    a. tell you that routine procedures are standardized and cannot be changed.
    b. tell you to try out the method to see whether it works.

c. discuss the suggestion with you and determine its value.

d. discuss the suggestion endlessly, probably with limited or no solution.

8. Let's say you're aspiring to a supervisory role or higher. If one of your subordinates does an exceptionally fine piece of work, it is usually best to . . .

a. praise him moderately so that he knows his efforts are appreciated.

b. say nothing so that he will not become conceited.

c. tell him that none of his peers could have done as fine a job as he did.

d. explain how the work could have been done even better.

9. Do you honestly feel that you are discriminated against? Has your race, religion, sex, or national origin been an impediment to your career progress?

a. yes

b. no

10. Last Christmas, we met Sharon while waiting for a plane in Austin, Texas. This is her story.

"Recently, I was promoted from a senior accounting clerk position to junior accountant. Now, I'm in the nonexempt category and don't get paid for overtime. While it's true I received a three-thousand dollar increase, it's also true I'm working a heck of a lot more hours.

In fact, I figured out that if I worked these extra hours in my former job, I'd be making much more money than I do now. I mentioned this to my supervisor and she said, 'It goes with the territory.'

"I'm not sure what, if anything, I can or should do. The only thing I know is I need some good advice. Can you help me?"

Which of the following advice would you have given Sharon if she had asked you instead?

a. "Politely, but firmly, explain to your boss that although you are not in a supervisory position, your time is valuable to you and perhaps a quick raise would take care of the situation."

b. "Moving from a nonprofessional position to a professional one means not watching the clock so closely. You may not immediately feel the benefits of your new job, but soon you'll be exposed to a wider range of career-advancement possibilities and opportunities for upward salary mobility."

c. "Suggest to your supervisor that she streamline your job somewhat. A snip here and a cut there in your responsibilities could save you time."

11. Do you often feel that your boss avoids or manipulates you by using jargon or double-talk . . . using plain words in such a way that you can't understand?

    a. yes
    b. no

12. "My boss frequently gives me dirty looks. Since I was hired (seven months ago) no one has said, 'Please do it this way. I'd prefer it.' I guess that would have been too simple, too direct. They tell me nothing to my face—instead, they talk about me behind my back saying what a lousy job I'm doing."

    a. That type of behavior occurs frequently where I work.
    b. That type of behavior doesn't occur where I work.

13. Nearly everyone wants feedback about their on-the-job performance, whether it is praise or constructive criticism. Employees frequently judge their boss by the way feedback is doled out. But these same employees often forget that the boss is also a human being. He or she needs feedback, too. The best assistants have discovered that just as they wish to be complimented for a job well done, so do their bosses.

    When was the last time you gave your boss positive feedback?

    a. within the past month
    b. within the past two weeks
    c. Never—that S.O.B. doesn't deserve it.

14. For whom do you work . . . a boss or a leader?

Bosses	Leaders
drive their people	coach others
inspire fear	inspire enthusiasm
say, "Get here on time."	get there ahead of time
say, "Go do it."	say, "Let's go to it."
use people	develop people

It seems I work for a _____.

    a. boss
    b. leader

15. Teamwork is definitely in fashion today. "Getting along" and being a "team player" often put people on the road to further promotions. The philosophy exists that when people from different disciplines and viewpoints are brought together, their decisions will better mirror company thinking. Also, these people collectively should be able to solve a broader scope of problems than they would as individuals working separately. However, teamwork is not for everyone. Not everyone views team-building as a panacea. How about you?

Do you feel that teamwork increases the amount of "red tape" needed to get something done?

    a. yes
    b. no

16. Do you feel unduly pressured to be a team member when you'd rather work alone?

    a. yes
    b. no
    c. does not apply

17. Does your company set up research teams and then give them insufficient authority to enact their conclusions?

    a. yes
    b. no
    c. does not apply

18. The opportunity to be visible and to be known by upper management can be crucial to your further success and on-the-job well-being. Realistically, your chances for advancement are diminished if your good work goes unnoticed.

    From your perspective, how well known are you for the good work you do?

    a. Many power people on all levels and departments know me.
    b. I'm relatively well known . . . better than most of my peers.
    c. I'm relatively unknown.
    d. Outside my immediate work area, nobody even knows I exist.

19. "I've already talked to my boss about it ten times," says Louise, an administrative assistant in a Fortune 500 company. "She gives me explicit directions that she doesn't want to talk to someone and then picks up the phone after I've said she's out. Or she has me get someone on the line for her and then leaves the office or picks up her private line and makes another call. She's so erratic, I don't know if I'm coming or going."

    Do you have similar complaints?

    a. yes
    b. no

20. How frequently are you asked for your opinion about the day-to-day operations in your department?

    a. Almost every time a question arises.
    b. Occasionally.
    c. Rarely.
    d. Come to think of it, never.

Kevin Gottlieb, who has a Ph.D. in political science, has held a variety of positions, often three at the same time, in politics, business and teaching. Former president of a national advertising association in Washington, D.C., Senior Policy Advisor for U.S. Senator Donald Riegle and professor in the Department of Social Science at Michigan State University, he is now Staff Director of the U.S. Senate Banking Committee.

Mr. Gottlieb strongly believes that people with adequate intelligence can, with exceptional hard work and disciplined behavior, achieve significantly, standing out when compared to others who might be brighter but don't want to work as hard. He admits that at times it would have been easier for him to have had just one job.

After all, it requires less time, and provides more time to pursue personal interests. But, as you will soon learn, that's not his style. At least, it hasn't been that way, since his first Stay or Leave job decision eighteen years ago. Ever since that time, he has let it be known: "If you want me to work for you, there's three things I want to do. I want to teach and do educational research. I want to be involved in the private sector and run a business. And I want to continue my work in politics and public policy. If you'll let me structure a career where I can do that then I'll come with you . . . otherwise, I appreciate the offer, I'm flattered, but, no thanks." Mr Gottlieb also warns: "If your only measure is how much money they're going to pay you, then you're up for sale to the highest bidder—period."

Mr. Gottlieb vividly recalls the first lesson he learned. The events set the pattern for who he is today, and why he thinks the way he does.

"I remember it very clearly when I made that decision to leave Syracuse University and go to Michigan State University. I was Assistant Vice-President for Governmental Affairs and Research for the university. In addition, I was Director of Environmental Affairs and Associate Director of the Office-Sponsored Programs.

"So, here I was, working along and trying to do the best I could with these two different positions when suddenly I learned my boss, the Vice-President of Governmental Affairs and Research, had differed fundamentally with the Chancellor of the university. The Chancellor eventually made the decision to eliminate the entire office in which I worked. Using this method, the decision would be viewed as organizational, not personal. So, on May 7, 1971, my colleagues and I were told we would have to leave the University by July 1. This was the first time in life that I had ever had someone tell me that I had to find something else.

"I immediately began to search for another position because I had no choice; or so I thought. I answered advertisements. I talked to colleagues at Syracuse and to those at other institutions. I then made numerous phone inquiries, and began interviewing for these various jobs.

"At one point, I received a call from the university saying, 'Look, we decided we didn't give you enough advance notice, so we're going to extend your contract from July 1 until September 1 to give you more time to find a new position.' I told them how much I appreciated their offer, but my continued interviewing produced three job offers from different universities. I chose the Michigan State University teaching position, which was not to start until September 1. Later Syracuse University called me in and said, 'We just found out we received these grants from the federal government. They're in your field and we would like you to be the one to stay and direct them.' I responded by saying, 'I really appreciate your interest in having me stay now. However, I have accepted a position at Michigan State University which I will begin after I have taken August off for my vacation.'

"Now, in a real sense, this is a stay or leave situation—because I have the opportunity to stay, be in charge of the two grants, not move my house, live comfortably in an environment I know well, while staying with friends, many of whom are remaining in Syracuse. Everything would have been easier if I had stayed at Syracuse.

"But I learned a dramatic lesson then at twenty-nine years of age. That lesson is: 'Institutions will inevitably do what's best for the institution at the expense of the individual, even though it will protest that people and their issues come first.' Only then, when the institution needed me to do something for it, did it think in terms of doing something for me. I had been delivering for them for years. But when they reached the point where they had another goal to achieve, they closed down the entire section as an organizational restructuring rather than an action directed at an individual. Now once I saw this behavior, it was not possible for me to consider staying to help them with their two grants.

"I learned another important lesson. Don't ever, under any circumstances, put your career eggs in one job basket. Don't ever work just one job. Work as many jobs as your physical condition will permit you to work. Don't ever accept a job with any one entity, without letting that entity know you are going to work also for others and you're going to carry on other dimensions of your career. If they say, 'Well, we want you to come work for us, but only for us, nobody else,' that job may be one you don't want to accept. Have as many different affiliations and jobs as you possibly can because two things will happen. First, you're always protected, because the affiliations cannot all have a problem at once. Second, each one of the affiliations respects you more if they know that the others are bidding for your time. Consequently, they treat you more seriously, more respectfully than they would if they thought you were totally under their control.

"This approach also gives you a special option. If any one of the institutions or affiliations asks you to do something illegal, immoral or unethical, you can say without anguish, without anxiety, 'In my judgment, you've asked me to do something that's illegal, unethical, and immoral; therefore, I'm leaving to work elsewhere.' Freedom of this sort is less likely if all you have is the one job affiliation."

Linda met Pat Roddy when he was confronted with a major Stay or Leave decision. The position of executive producer at ABC News was pending. Six months later we're happy to say Mr. Roddy is Executive Producer at ABC News in New York. Here is his story about a Stay or Leave situation he faced earlier in his career.

"Two weeks before I graduated from college, I started working as an engineer at ABC.

"After three years on the job, I was ready to move up into the producing area. But it took two more years before anyone would listen. At that time, this type of move was unheard of. Engineering was engineering, news was news. They didn't get along—they didn't mix. That's the way it was.

"However, Sam Donaldson and News Executive Producer Dorrance Smith thought it was a good idea and things began to happen until it became a question of staying in engineering or venturing into producing. I decided to stay with ABC yet go into a whole new career—producing.

"Then came the advice, 'You can't associate with the same people anymore. You're not one of them any longer and you have to be sure they understand it and you understand it. Otherwise you won't succeed.' I didn't play that game. I made up my own rules. All I knew was that it was very important not to come across that I'm better than my former colleagues because I have ascended. And at the same time, I had to make sure my new colleagues looked at me in the right light.

"It was a situation of forming new associations without saying to the others, 'You don't matter anymore.' "

Whether it's innate or learned, your ability to properly handle company politics can dictate your survival on the job, and often regulates your upward mobility. But we all have different capacities. What appears to be a threatening situation to one person is mere child's play to another. Questions 21 through 25 ask you to rate yourself.

21. Are you able to recognize a politically charged situation before it explodes?

    a. almost always
    b. only sometimes
    c. hardly ever

22. Can you identify the players and who aligns with whom?

    a. almost always
    b. only sometimes
    c. hardly ever

23. Do you know how to defuse a politically dangerous situation in which you're involved?

    a. almost always
    b. only sometimes
    c. hardly ever

24. If you find yourself stuck between two competing factions, can you find a way out?

    a. almost always
    b. only sometimes
    c. hardly ever

25. Do you enjoy and have the stomach for the games of company politics?

    a. almost always
    b. only sometimes
    c. hardly ever

General employee morale is an important consideration in your evaluation of your company's potential. The overall internal social climate frequently influences a company's progress and consequently can influence your professional progress. Morale is not an easily measured characteristic, but there are subtle clues that can help you size up the current situation. Questions 26 through 32 explore some of these clues.

26. Do you and many of your coworkers choose to use the product or service your company provides over a competitor's?

    a. yes
    b. no

27. Generally speaking, would you say most employees in your department enjoy their work—or do they discontentedly punch the nine-to-five time clock?

    a. enjoy their work
    b. punch the time clock

28. Are the company's goals clearly delineated and made known by top management?

    a. yes
    b. no

Bob Woodward is the Assistant Managing Editor of the investigative unit at the Washington Post. He joined the Post in 1971 and, with Carl Bernstein, investigated the break-in at the Democratic Headquarters in the Watergate office building. Woodward and Bernstein coauthored two best-selling books, All the President's Men and The Final Days. Mr. Woodward also wrote Wired and VEIL: The Secret Wars of the CIA 1981–1987.

Linda's Day-Timer® showed it took two months at the rate of two or three phone calls per week to finally sense Bob Woodward's friendly smile the day he said, "Linda, you're the most persistent person I have ever met; come on in."

"Stay or leave? That's a good subject. I came to the Post in September 1971. Carl Bernstein and I did the Watergate story, we did a couple of books and then I worked as the Metropolitan Editor. I'd been here eleven years and I was back doing some reporting when I got a call from CBS. Vance Sauter, Ed Joyce and Dan Rather offered me a job as a reporter. They did an effective job of saying, 'Look, television is where the action is, not newspaper writing, not book writing. We will give you a license to do anything you want. You will have a camera crew to go around and do for CBS what you've done for the Post for the past eleven years. We'll pay four times as much as you're getting from the Post.'

"The first thing in stay or leave is: who do you include in making that decision? Do you make it by yourself, do you go for a walk in the forest or on the beach? Do you consult your wife or girlfriend? I decided to make it broad. I included friends and eventually my boss here at the Post. I went to Ben Bradlee, the Editor of the Post, and said, 'I've got an offer to go to CBS, this is what it is, and I've got to tell you I'm seriously considering it. I have not decided. This place has become part of my family and I don't make decisions without the total family members.' He said, 'We don't want you to leave.' He talked to some people. He wrote me a letter. It said part of the soul of this place will go if you leave. You shouldn't do it for your own sake, you won't be that good at it. He had a gentle way about him. You're not that good on television. He said that it would be bad for the Post. Bad for newspaper work. In a nice tactful way, he said it would be a misdirection, a bit of a sellout to the glitzier side of journalism. He said they would pay me whatever I wanted. They would create this investigative unit . . . I'd have my own staff, be able to choose my subject . . . would give me a great deal of latitude.

"He then enlisted Donald Graham, the publisher of the paper, to take me out to lunch. Everyone likes to be told they're needed and wanted. What was nice, Bradlee did the 'good cop' routine, then

Graham took me out to lunch. Not that he was a 'bad cop' about it—he said the same things. 'Don't do it. It wouldn't be good for you, for the paper.' But he also had a way of saying, 'Look! You do your reporting, you do it fairly well. You do it as well as anyone, you have perfected a method and it's paid off.' He asked me what I wanted to be when I grew up? I said I wasn't sure—that's why I was thinking of this CBS offer. He then proceeded to tell me I was not ten feet tall, yet I was very good at what I did. That I was not going to end up as the editor of the paper, almost certainly that was not going to happen. 'You're more useful to the paper and to yourself as a reporter,' he said. 'At the same time we want to keep you, if you want to take time to write a book, we will be flexible. These are your opportunities and limits and don't go to TV.' This would be like my colleague during the Watergate incident. Carl Bernstein had left. A number of others had left to go from print to television. He said, 'Take the long view and take a moment to take stock of what you can and can't do.' A lot of people I spoke to said 'Go to CBS, take a new challenge, do something different . . . take on a new role . . . don't get stale.'

"I looked around and rethought it and came to the conclusion to stay. I couldn't leave the place where I grew up. They had taken great risks with me during the Watergate story. I feel that newspapers matter. They live beyond what goes over the airways.

"In the process of talking to people, I was able to make the decision on reason, the flexibility of the institution and the emotional family. I've learned how untrained we are to make decisions like that. You have to systematize it. You have to sample opinions. It forced me to come to grips with some values. The values are family affiliations in your job. When you go someplace new, they don't know you or your weaknesses or strengths. I have a lot of good will in the bank here. If I have a bad year or screw up or don't work very hard and so forth, there would be some give. So I knew I had that, a cushion here. You go someplace else and you start on Monday, by Friday it's 'What have you done for us this week?'

"So I realized that I was a little fearful of change. It's easy to look back in retrospect and say I'm really glad I stayed, that CBS has gone through some real difficult times with cutbacks. They're generally not interested in the kind of stories I do. It would have been exactly the wrong time to go there. If you read *Who Killed CBS?* you will most likely agree there was a lot of energy in CBS that went into office politics and jockeying around and probably not enough into quality of the journalistic product.

"I was lucky. How easy it is to make bad decisions."

29. If your answer to the previous question was "No," skip this question. If your answer was "Yes," would you say that the majority of employees support the goals of top management?

    a. yes
    b. no

30. Part of the morale picture is painted by the quality of the rewards employees receive. Do you think that most of your coworkers feel that they are properly compensated (in terms of pay, benefits, recognition and promotions) for the services they are performing?

    a. yes
    b. no

31. Even in the best organizations, some office politicking, including the formation of cliques, is inevitable. If the general morale is upbeat, then a healthy spirit of competitiveness and challenges among offices or divisions ensues. If, however, morale is low, the same cliques engage in backstabbing, creating injurious collisions and ruthless encounters. Such an environment is not the best one in which to develop your career. As you see it, would you say that morale at your current workplace is relatively . . .

    a. high?
    b. low?

32. High turnover is often a telltale sign of low morale and a company's lack of commitment to its employees. If seasoned veterans are among those who leave, who will be left to help you improve your skills and abilities?

    Is your company experiencing higher turnover than comparable companies in your industry?

    a. yes
    b. no
    c. I don't know. I guess I should find out.

33. By definition, groups of any kind try to get their members to conform. This holds true for the workplace, whether it's an office, factory or store. Which of the following brief descriptions most nearly fits your workplace?

    A. An informal worksite that appears to have a friendly, family-type atmosphere. Group members share their feelings, personal stories and family tidbits. A sense of security pervades as most workers know almost everything about each other.

    B. A formal worksite, quite typical of large, conventional organizations. Here the group members may form teams to complete tasks but do not openly share the events of their personal lives. Their competence, or lack of it, speaks for them.

C. An informal worksite that exerts pressure on members of the group to prove their loyalty by revealing personal matters. Power struggles are commonplace and workers tend to lean the way the wind is currently blowing strongest.

Which description comes closest to your present situation. Is it A, B or C? Think about it. Okay, now the important question: Is this where you would like to spend the next few years?

    a.   yes
    b.   no

34. Simply put: Lately, has your boss been able to look you straight in the eye?

    a.   yes
    b.   no

35. Sandra, a salesperson, says, "My boss keeps making my job tougher and tougher. She keeps raising my quotas and throwing other obstacles in my way. At first, I though her tactics were just a training technique, but lately she acts as if I'm out for her job."

    Are you in a similar situation?

    a.   yes
    b.   no

36. One way to get a sense of the qualifications needed for a position a level or two above yours is to take several persons at that level out to lunch, one at a time. During lunch, you can "interview" them, make new friends, and get some idea of their accomplishments and the specific tasks they perform. Then try to determine if they are more political than you . . . more socially skilled.

    Have you done this recently?

    a.   yes
    b.   no

37. Is this you? "I have discussed my personal life with too many people at work. Now I'm vulnerable. I will have to be more close-mouthed and learn to keep things to myself."

    a.   That's me!
    b.   That's not me.

38. Which of the following describes your current situation?

    a. Your boss really doesn't know what he's doing.

    b. You're the only one your boss complains about.

    c. Your boss provides a structured environment that helps you function successfully.

    d. None of the above.

39. You know how to do your job very well, but the supervisor occasionally peers over your shoulder and checks out your performance. How do you react?

    a. You welcome these occasions to show that you really know what you're doing and have developed certain "shortcuts." Then you ask your supervisor for his reaction.

    b. First you become very nervous and make more mistakes than usual. Then you dig up excuses for your poor performance. At this point, your supervisor ridicules these excuses and a conflict begins.

    c. You have become oblivious to these occurrences. You have your job to do, and he has his.

    d. None of the above.

40. Let's assume you're an above-average employee. You do what is expected of you and frequently go beyond. But because you're only human, you occasionally make a mistake. When this happens, your boss . . .

    a. criticizes you in front of others.

    b. avoids talking to you for a week and then, when he does talk to you, his conversation is threatening and sarcastic.

    c. acknowledges your error and makes suggestions in private.

    d. none of the above.

41. Sometimes we fool ourselves. We believe what we want to believe. We think our relationship with the boss is a win-win situation; but it's not. Or we think we're at odds, and we're mistaken again.

    One way to test your relationship with your boss is to request an opportunity to attend educational seminars or training workshops. To date, which of the following best describes your actions/your boss's reactions?

    a. You have repeatedly requested to take company-sponsored training sessions. Your requests have been denied each time.

    b. Your company does not have in-house workshops. You have repeatedly requested to attend local, state or national conferences related to your area of expertise. Your requests have been denied.

    c. You have not requested the opportunity to attend training sessions or workshops. You plan to do so soon.

    d. Your boss encourages or permits you to attend a fair share of seminars and workshops.

42. When you do an assigned task exceptionally well, do you get the feeling your boss appreciates what you have done?

    a. occasionally
    b. often
    c. rarely
    d. does not apply

43. Generally speaking, your immediate supervisor . . .

    a. listens to your suggestions but does not have the power to enact changes.
    b. is jealous of your talents.
    c. tends to procrastinate in the decision-making process.
    d. none of the above.

44. Think back to the last time you volunteered to do something that is not part of your typical job description. If you did it well, were you given the feeling that your extra effort was appreciated?

    a. yes
    b. no
    c. I have never volunteered.

45. Good bosses can mean the difference between a career that succeeds and one that doesn't. Here are six characteristics of a good boss.

- Encourages you to set goals.
- Lets you know he or she is listening, and has confidence in you.
- Allows you to complete your work without interference (such as idle chatter or frequent changes in the assignment).
- Motivates more with praise than with criticism.
- Sets definite, yet reasonable, guidelines and allows suggestions to bounce freely within these broad boundaries.
- Gives you a second chance when you goof up.

How many of these characteristics does your boss exhibit?

    a. none or one
    b. two or three
    c. four or five
    d. all six

46. Many careers have become extremely specialized. This narrow scope can lead to boredom. As a counteractive measure, a well-meaning supervisor can expand your role in an attempt to make your job more interesting. Has your boss . . .

    a. added more complexity to the tasks you perform?
    b. raised your quota by adding identical tasks?
    c. trained you to handle more than one job?
    d. done none of the above?

Now Vice-Chairman and Member of the Office of Chief Executive of MCI Communications Corporation, V. Orville Wright spent twenty years working at IBM. At IBM, he felt limited to a fairly narrow range of management having to do with sales and marketing. Mr. Wright wanted to broaden his knowledge and experience, become a general manager and one day run his own company. So when he reached the point of boredom, wondering what he was still doing there, he said, "I quit."

When asked, "What do you know about yourself today that you didn't know when you first started out?," he answered:

"If I learned anything over the time it was how much there was left to know in the operation of a company. I learned that if you have a plan and if you know what you're trying to do, then moving from job to job probably furthers your career (if yours is not the case [if you don't have a clear plan and goal] then doing the same thing can cause you more harm). Some people would say I did a lot of job hopping.

"Working for large organizations has given me a lot of empathy for people. I like people, genuinely like people. I feel the only way a company can be successful is to be very fair with its people. Let all the people in the company share success but at the same time hold everyone, regardless of what they do, somewhat responsible for fulfilling their assigned roles."

Okay, so you think you're experiencing a personality clash with your supervisor. That does not mean you should immediately pack your suitcase and brush up on your interviewing skills. Questions 47 through 52 help you evaluate this situation.

47. Are you in top management and is your supervisor president of the company?

    a. yes
    b. no

48. Does your supervisor have the power to sever your employment?

    a. yes
    b. no

49. Is your clash with a newly appointed superior who has just replaced your former mentor?

    a. yes
    b. no

50. Criticism from your boss doesn't necessarily mean a personality clash exists. Are you sure this is what you're experiencing and not just a difference of opinion?

    a. yes
    b. no

51. Getting along with your boss is a two-way street. Of course it's important how he treats you, but equally important is the effort you make to understand his current position. He too has a boss and must be held accountable.

    Which of the following statements best describes your relationship with your boss?

    a. You've given it your all. You have adjusted to your boss's side each time he shifts his position and have clearly demonstrated your personal support. However, it seems that your extreme loyalty is misinterpreted as an inability to have a mind of your own. Unfortunately, the outcome is that you're used as a scapegoat or a doormat.

    b. You've noticed that your boss is unpredictable and usually disorganized—constantly preoccupied with petty problems. You have tried to relieve him of these minor worries but your actions have only created more tension.

    c. You've made it a point to see that your boss gets the credit, honor, and glory whenever things go right. In your gut you've realized that the part you play is important, perhaps vital. But you have not tried to hog the credit.

    d. None of the above.

52. Performance appraisals, if conducted properly, can provide an excellent opportunity for you and your boss to improve your relationship by clarifying what each expects of the other. Do you and your boss get together on a regularly scheduled basis (monthly, quarterly, semiannually, or even annually) to set specific goals and evaluate your performance?

    a. yes
    b. no

53. You cannot expect your boss to recall every contribution you've made to your organization. To facilitate the evaluative process, do you keep and present an accurate record, perhaps a list, calendar or diary of your accomplishments?

    a. Yes.
    b. No, but I should.
    c. No—I'm positive that son-of-a-gun wouldn't bother to look at it.
    d. No, we don't have evaluation meetings.

54. The majority of your coworkers are ———.

    a. friendly
    b. cooperative
    c. secretive
    d. backstabbing

Values/Skills Test

1. The following list contains thirty-two commonly held job-related values. As you go through the list, you will discover that you'll instinctively feel some are more important than others for your overall job satisfaction.

Select the six values that currently hold the most attraction and meaning for you.

1. _____   4. _____

2. _____   5. _____

3. _____   6. _____

Value	*Work-related Definition*
Above-average income	Doing work that will probably result in the accumulation of large amounts of money.
Adventure	Taking risks as a part of my work.
Artistic expression	Working as a painter, sculptor or composer, or in some other artistically creative occupation.
Beauty	Studying and appreciating beauty—things, words, ideas, etc.—as a normal part of my work.
Belonging	Feeling I can be recognized as a member of an organization or group as a result of my work.
Change	Working in an environment that involves constant change and the performance of many different tasks.
Community involvement	Working in a location that permits me to be involved as a member of the community.
Competition	Being involved in work in which my abilities are pitted against those of others.
Contact with people	Having day-to-day contact with the public as part of my work.
Creativity	Coming up with new ideas or ways of doing things as a normal part of my work.

Excitement	Working in an environment that is exciting.
Fast pace	Having a work environment in which things happen quickly and continuously.
Flexibility	Working according to my own time schedule.
Helping others	Helping other people directly—either one-to-one or in a small group.
Helping society	Doing things that help make the world a better place.
Independence	Being able to decide for myself what needs to be done; not having to take orders from someone else.
Influencing people	Doing work that involves trying to influence the way people act or the opinions that they have.
Knowledge	Being involved in work that explores basic truth and understanding.
Location	Working in a location that allows me to pursue the leisure activities I enjoy most.
Making decisions	Forming policies or choosing courses of action as part of my work.
Mental challenge	Being involved in work requiring thinking and analyzing.
Moral fulfillment	Doing work which contributes to the advancement of moral standards that I feel are important.
Physical challenge	Performing a job that requires physical strength and stamina.
Power	Exercising authority over the work of others.
Precision	Working in an environment where there is little room for error.
Recognition	Being recognized by others for my work.
Security	Working where there is an adequate salary and little possibility of being laid off or getting fired.
Stability	Doing work that involves the performance of tasks that are similar from day to day.
Supervision	Being responsible for the work done by others.

Working alone	Working by myself, with little contact with others.
Working under pressure	Working in an environment in which there is pressure to get things done.
Working with others	Working as a member of a team or group.

How many of the six values you selected does your present job satisfy?

a. six
b. five
c. four or three
d. two or one
e. none

To complete questions 2 through 7, you'll need a couple of blank sheets of paper. Get them and we'll meet you here when you return.

Ready? Let's go.

Start by outlining your autobiography. Summarize the milestones in your life and whether they have had a positive or negative effect on you. Include, if appropriate, your relationship with your parents, siblings, peers and teachers. You might also want to include part-time jobs you've held, travel experiences, social conditions you experienced in your neighborhood, and sports and hobbies, along with major accomplishments or major disappointments.

If they are applicable and important, include experiences such as marriage, raising children and the death of a friend or loved one. If certain events on previous jobs are important, include them too. List whatever is important to you.

Now, if you haven't already done so, put these milestones, experiences and events (and their impact on you) into chronological order. Reread your listing. *Try to dismiss the fact that it is about you. Instead, let your imagination go and make believe this is an outline of a fictional character in a novel.* Answer questions 2 through 7 based upon what you read in this listing.

2. Do you find this character interesting?

    a. yes
    b. no

3. Do you think this character is capable of more responsibility than he or she has?

    a. yes
    b. no

Art Buchwald is the author of over thirty books, a columnist whose work appears in over five hundred newspapers and the recipient of the Pulitzer Prize for "outstanding commentary" in 1982.

Surely most of you will agree that "Life is a decision." Ask Mr. Buchwald and he won't hesitate to tell you his thoughts on that subject:

"All the decisions you make in life have a tremendous luck factor. I remember when I was a kid looking for a job. I went to Paramount Pictures one day after school, and I saw John O'Connor, the personnel manager. I said, 'Father Murphy sent me.' And I got the job!

"I am motivated by always wanting to do better. It's not like I could quit because I proved it to myself . . . so that's why the job never gets boring and I never get old. Because I don't have the attitude 'I have it made.'

"You have to know how to make decisions. . . . Life is a decision, writing a book is a decision. . . . But the greatest decision I ever made in life was when I was going to USC after World War II. I was in my third year and someone came up to me and said, 'Do you know you could go to Paris on the GI Bill of Rights?' And I said, 'I didn't know that—but if that's the truth, I'm going.' And I did.

"It changed my whole life because I stayed there for fourteen years. I married, had a family, and my professional career began there.

"Everything I am today came out of that experience . . . that one decision . . . not staying in California."

4. Do you think this character should be paid more than he or she currently earns?

    a. yes
    b. no

5. Do you think this character has the personal skills to reach for a higher-level position?

    a. yes
    b. no

6. Does this character exhibit the values you most admire?

    a. yes
    b. no

7. Which of the following phrases best describes this character's history, decisions, feelings and philosophy?

a. Don't rock the boat.
b. Reach for the stars.
c. Look before you leap.

8. Although none of these brief descriptions may exactly fit you, select the one that best describes your outlook.

a. "I don't feel about my job the same way I did when I first started. Now, I know the ropes and tend to coast more often."
b. "I've learned there's more to life than just work. I'm older and have developed some outside interests that satisfy me. I'd say that my job isn't as important as it used to be."
c. "Although others may feel that ambitious people should not be trusted and that ambition is not an admirable quality, I can honestly say I have an 'onward-and-upward' outlook on life. Ambition is the stuff that fuels my dreams."

9. Leaving your current position and going into another usually entails some risk. Which of the following statements best exemplifies your attitude toward risk-taking?

a. I enjoy the adventure associated with taking risks.
b. I'll risk and even if I fail, I'll still learn from it.
c. I'll avoid taking a risk now. Perhaps something even better will come along.

10. How would you feel if you had to continue working in your present occupational field for the rest of your life?

a. Great, it's what I want.
b. Okay, for now. But I'm keeping my eyes and ears open to other possibilities.
c. I've come to realize this is not my field.

11. Those who work in fields that serve basic needs of the public enjoy the greatest geographic mobility. Teachers, salespeople, nurses, secretaries and general-practice lawyers, for example, can usually find employment almost anywhere in the nation. However, the more specialized your occupation, the more likely you may be limited to specific areas. Interested in publishing? You'll need to spend some time in New York or Los Angeles. Oil industry technician? It's off to Texas, Oklahoma or Alaska for a while.

Did you seriously take into account your geographic location when you accepted your current position?

a. yes
b. no

12. Are you happy with the geographic location of your current job?

    a. yes
    b. no

13. Is your current location at the top of your list?

    a. yes
    b. no

14. Does your company have other offices or worksites you could transfer to, if you desired?

    a. yes
    b. no

15. Since you are taking this test, you're probably not in your "dream job." You know, the one with all your ultimate personal satisfiers—filled only with the tasks and activities you really want to do.

    What's more likely is that you're currently in a series of stepping-stone jobs, each increasing your skill level or helping you gain necessary experience. Do you consider your current job . . .

    a. very close to your dream job; one with just a few minor factors that annoy you?
    b. a stepping-stone job; one in a series of jobs that may ultimately lead you to your dream job?

16. All things considered, if a friend were interested in a job like mine, I would _____ him/her.

    a. encourage
    b. discourage

17. People differ in the amount of variety they require. Some go every weekend to the same restaurant; others try never to go to the same place twice. On the job, it's the same. Some people say, "My job keeps me plenty busy, but I'm still bored," while others announce, "I've got so many different things to do, I sometimes forget which hat I'm wearing."

    Does the amount of variety you get on the job suit your current needs?

    a. yes
    b. no

18. My job could be a heck of a lot better if there were hope for _____.

    a. advancement
    b. more freedom to do what I please
    c. substantially increased earnings

d. learning and doing new things
e. two of the above
f. three or four of the above

19. Have you viewed your values lately? Chances are you would not be alone if a few years ago you chose a career without considering your personal values. And even if you did take them into account, your current values may be different. Times change, you change, and so do your values. Select your most important value from each of the following sets (A, B and C).

Set A

- *Action*—being employed in an environment where decisions need to be made quickly and frequently.
- *Creativity*—discovering new and innovative ways of doing things as a usual everyday pattern.
- *Precision*—working in an atmosphere that allows little room for error.
- *Stability*—performing tasks that are similar from day to day.

Set A, most important: _____.

Set B

- *Mental challenge*—engaging in work that requires considerable analyzing and abstract thinking.
- *Physical challenge*—accomplishing tasks that require physical strength and stamina.
- *Location*—working in a surrounding that allows me to pursue the leisure-time activities I enjoy most.
- *Moral fulfillment*—promoting and advancing the moral standards I feel are important.

Set B, most important: _____.

Set C

- *Competition*—working in an environment in which my results are constantly pitted against those of my peers.
- *Cohesiveness*—working as a member of a team that is highly interdependent.
- *Independence*—having little contact with people; working alone.
- *Power*—having authority over and responsibility for the work of others.

Set C, most important: _____.

My current job satisfies . . .

a. all three I selected.
b. two I selected.
c. only one I selected.
d. none of those I selected.

Charlie Byrd, the classical and jazz guitarist, has won virtually every major award available to a guitarist and has toured the world for the U.S Department of State. Willis Conover of the Voice of America has said of his achievements: "Charlie Byrd's versatility in the literature of the guitar surpasses that of anyone else. He is a masterful jack of all guitar trades."

It was on a Saturday night in Georgetown at Blues Alley, one of the last regular venues for top jazz performers in the D.C. area, that Byrd dedicated these notes to Stay or Leave. Byrd has apparently made an obsessive decision to stay, *no matter what:*

"There have been several ups and downs in my career. But I always knew what I wanted to do and I don't intend to change now. I have a lot of stick-to-it-ivness. Sure I see more airports than anyone should have to see and I sleep in more hotel rooms than I would like to. But that's the price I have to pay to find an audience. I want to perform!"

20. A bona fide promotion within your company or department can be an example of simultaneously staying and leaving. You'll stay in familiar territory where you know the players, rules, company benefits, etc.; you'll leave the familiarity of your old job and take on new duties, responsibilities and experiences.

    Sounds good.

    Let's continue. Our investigations suggest that if you can successfully handle eight out of ten tasks that your supervisor performs, you most likely are ready to move up a rung on the ladder.

    Although you can handle the specific tasks and activities a promotion will bring, the big question remains: Do you want to do what your supervisor does now?

    a. yes
    b. no

21. Below are three lists of work-related values. Select the *one* list (A, B or C) that best coincides with your present thinking. It is now important for me to . . .

    ### List A

    take on dangerous tasks if they interest me.
    be recognized for my work.
    work where my abilities are pitted against those of others.
    work in an environment I find exciting.

List B

have a secure position.
work where my tasks are similar each day.
know that my efforts are appreciated.
feel I am treated like everyone else at work.

List C

work in a way that makes the world a better place.
find pleasure in the beauty of my work.
advance the moral standards I feel are important.
work in a group rather than by myself.

My choice is _____ (A, B or C).

How many of the four items in your selected list are being met by your current job?

    a. four
    b. three
    c. two
    d. one
    e. none

22. Your job can have a strong impact on your personal relationships. The amount of time you spend and the intensity of your work are two common, often negative, components that lead to job dissatisfaction and the desire to leave.

    Truthfully now, are you so tense after a day's work that you are often grouchy and nasty when you arrive home?

    a. yes
    b. no

23. Do you have enough time to pursue a hobby or sport, if you want to?

    a. yes
    b. no

24. Do you find that when you're away from your workplace, all you can think of is what needs to be done when you return?

    a. yes
    b. no

25. Do you feel guilty when you take a vacation?

    a. yes
    b. no

Interview
Alan Cranston
U.S. Senator

A senator since 1969, Alan Cranston was recently unanimously elected to a sixth term as the Democratic party whip. He is chairman of the Veterans' Affairs Committee, the Subcommittee on Housing and Urban Affairs and the Subcommittee on East Asian and Pacific Affairs.

"Probably my most significant stay or leave decision came while fulfilling my original life's ambition as a foreign correspondent. After graduating from Stanford University, I was covering the Nazi atrocities and the evil actions in Italy.

"I decided I didn't want to spend my life recording such sorrowful events. I needed to be involved perhaps in heading them off. So I quit journalism and entered politics. That decision led me on the path to my position as a U.S. Senator."

---

26. Okay, you're employed and you're good at what you do. How long do you think you'll be satisfied doing the work you're doing?

    a. A couple of years.
    b. Six more months.
    c. I'm not satisfied.
    d. Many years.

Questions 27 and 28 refer to the following chart. To help you identify what is important to you and whether your unrest is due to a difference between what you perceive you need versus what you perceive you get, complete the chart by checking the appropriate "Importance" column and designating whether your job fulfills each need.

What Do I Need (Value)?	*How Important Is This?*			*Does My Job Fulfill This Need?*	
	Very	*Somewhat*	*Little*	*Yes*	*No*
1. Sufficient monetary rewards.	____	____	____	____	____
2. A boss who knows what he or she is doing.	____	____	____	____	____
3. An opportunity to advance my skills.	____	____	____	____	____

4. Social contacts. _____ _____ _____ _____ _____

5. An opportunity to help _____ _____ _____ _____ _____
   others.

6. A chance to travel. _____ _____ _____ _____ _____

7. An appropriate title. _____ _____ _____ _____ _____

8. Recognition for a job _____ _____ _____ _____ _____
   well done.

9. Doing what others find _____ _____ _____ _____ _____
   nearly impossible to
   do.

10. Working with my _____ _____ _____ _____ _____
    hands.

11. Direct contact with _____ _____ _____ _____ _____
    customers.

12. More influence on my _____ _____ _____ _____ _____
    job description.

13. Maximum leisure time. _____ _____ _____ _____ _____

14. Excitement caused by _____ _____ _____ _____ _____
    deadlines.

27. How many of the fourteen values do you consider Very Important?
_____ How many of these does your current job fulfill?

    a. all of them
    b. about half of them
    c. less than half of them

28. How many of the fourteen values do you consider Somewhat Important?
_____ How many of these does your current job fulfill?

    a. all of them
    b. about half of them
    c. less than half of them

Now President and Chief Executive Officer of MTV Networks, Tom Freston spent a good deal of time learning where in the world of work he would be happiest. His first job certainly wasn't his favorite:

"In 1970, I worked on the Procter & Gamble account at Benton and Bowles. Prell Concentrate and Scope Mouthwash were hard products to get behind emotionally. I found the advertising business a very slow business. Most of my time was spent grinding out numbers and reports and writing very formulaic letters back to a client testing a product in a test market for three or four years. Even if you elect to move one word in a TV commercial—that doesn't change its value one iota. We were spending six million dollars a year on mouthwash advertising, it was an acknowledged fact that mouthwash doesn't work, and the advertising was basically to drive paranoia into people to tell them that with bad breath they could lose their jobs and then we would offer them a product that didn't have any efficiency. It was like a lot of dangerous minds harmlessly occupied. It was not really fulfilling . . . meeting after meeting. I became totally disinterested, I became alienated, I just couldn't believe that this was what I wanted to do with my life. It was, however, a place with good training and discipline, and it was the only place I learned how to write business communications. I remember being threatened with a transfer to Charmin toilet paper . . . the ass-end of the advertising business. I actually did studies of people's toilet paper usage patterns and divided everyone in America into rollers, folders and crumplers. This was a famous research study where I found that a crumpler was a high-anxiety type person who was more likely to live in a city than in a rural area, and used 20 percent more toilet paper because he or she was always in a rush.

"I had a girl call me up from Paris one morning and say, 'Why don't you quit your job and come see me.' And I said, 'That's crazy.' And I did just that. I never regretted that decision to leave."

29. "I've been with this company for nine years and my responsibilities have steadily increased. However, my salary increases have not kept pace with my increasing responsibilities. Sure, I started with a fairly decent wage, but now I feel my pay is lower than it should be."

    a. That's me, more or less.
    b. That's not me. My pay is quite good.
    c. That's not me. My pay is really inadequate.

30. Companies do not hire people, nor do companies promote people; only people hire and promote other people! Therefore, to improve your current situation, you will have to take some interpersonal risks. You'll need to get out there and meet new people, recontact former friends and acquaintances, and interview with potential employers.
    At this time, are you prepared to do all this?

    a. yes
    b. no

31. Are you fairly confident that the skills you've acquired would keep you employable in relatively bad economic times?

    a. yes
    b. no

32. Can you name five other career fields you could enter wherein your current and prior experience would be relevant and valuable to your new employer?

    a. Yes, I can.
    b. No, I cannot.

33. Susan is a bright, talented, imaginative and energetic person who wants to go into business for herself. She recognizes her chance for success would increase if she hired an assistant who is . . .

    a. bright, talented, imaginative and energetic.
    b. dull and plodding, but honest.
    c. brilliant, yet conceited, self-centered and lazy.

Questions 34 through 37 refer to the list below, which contains seventy-eight personal skills and characteristics. In all likelihood, you possess nearly all of them to a degree, but some more than others. Look over the list and mark the ten that describe you best.

Personal Skills
Personal skills and characteristics affect the way we get along. As you identify them, do not compare yourself to others . . . just compare within yourself.

_____ Accurate	_____ Firm	_____ Physically strong
_____ Adventuresome	_____ Flexible	_____ Pleasant
_____ Alert	_____ Friendly	_____ Poised
_____ Ambitious	_____ Generous	_____ Polite
_____ Analytical	_____ Genuine	_____ Professional
_____ Artistic	_____ Hard working	_____ Punctual
_____ Assertive	_____ Honest	_____ Reliable
_____ Aware	_____ Imaginative	_____ Resourceful
_____ Calm	_____ Independent	_____ Responsible
_____ Capable	_____ Ingenious	_____ Self-controlled
_____ Common-sense	_____ Knowledgeable	_____ Self-reliant
_____ Conscientious	_____ Logical	_____ Self-starter
_____ Considerate	_____ Loyal	_____ Sense of humor
_____ Cooperative	_____ Mature	_____ Sensitive
_____ Courageous	_____ Mentally healthy	_____ Sincere
_____ Creative	_____ Methodical	_____ Spontaneous
_____ Curious	_____ Neat	_____ Supportive
_____ Dependable	_____ Open	_____ Sympathetic
_____ Diplomatic	_____ Open-minded	_____ Tactful
_____ Dynamic	_____ Optimistic	_____ Thorough
_____ Easygoing	_____ Orderly	_____ Tidy
_____ Emotionally stable	_____ Outgoing	_____ Tolerant
_____ Empathetic	_____ Patient	_____ Versatile
_____ Energetic	_____ Persistent	_____ Well groomed
_____ Enthusiastic	_____ Personable	_____ Well organized
_____ Expressive	_____ Physically healthy	_____ Willing to work

34. Let's imagine you have the responsibility for hiring your replacement. You've read her resume, checked references and completed the interview process. You determine her most outstanding skills are the same as the ten you selected above.

Based solely on her skills, what would you do?

    a. Hire her; the job and she are a great match.
    b. Not hire her; you suspect she will soon become bored with the job.
    c. Not hire her; you suspect the job-related tasks are beyond her current strengths.
    d. Hire her; she will learn from this job now and someday be ready to move upward.
    e. Not hire her; her personal skills do not fit the culture of this company.

35. How many of the skills you selected on your list are required to successfully accomplish the specific tasks of your job?

    a. all ten
    b. seven to nine
    c. four to six
    d. three or fewer

36. When you exhibit one or more of your skills and successfully complete a most difficult task, are you complimented or rewarded by your boss or peers?

    a. yes
    b. no

37. Select three more skills from the list, but this time choose the three which you most feel need definite improvement.

    1. _____

    2. _____

    3. _____

Does your current job, in some way, offer you the opportunity to improve these skills? Think it over.

    a. yes
    b. no
    c. yes, but not all three

It was 11:00 P.M., at Mutual Broadcasting in Arlington, Virginia. The "King," Larry King, was rapping up some news spots, and from the look of things he would have plenty of energy left for the minicassette recorder placed in front of him.

"The most important decision I ever had to make in my career recently happened.

"The word was out—my contract with CNN was going to end in June, 1988. I started hearing from others. ABC wanted me to follow Ted Koppel every night for an hour doing about the same thing I do for CNN but for a lot more money. And then King World, which distributes Oprah and Wheel of Fortune, came to us with an idea of syndicating 'The Larry King Show' every night for an enormous amount of money including a piece of the action. So, naturally CNN offered us more money to stay.

"Next came the dilemma of riches. The most money was offered by King World—the lowest, CNN. Among the three, nothing was under seven hundred thousand. To make things even more difficult, King World presented a position of ownership. ABC gave us a network position and CNN gave us something where we're comfortable.

"A major decision to make. I decided to stay at CNN. Ted Turner's offer was the lowest of the three. I got a five-year guaranteed contract. I went for comfort. It's at nine o'clock live when I have a special niche. I've meant a lot to the cable industry. It's been a nice marriage.

"So if I had a rule of thumb, it's this: Don't leave just for the money. If I had made a decision based on money alone—I think I would have lived to regret it. My decision was based upon happiness. It was also at the time I had open heart surgery.

"To think I could have made two million a year with King World alone . . . could have quit radio and done just an hour a day. Now I'm making over one million but doing two jobs. And at that level I don't know how much difference that is.

"Now, I was with Bill Cosby during this dickering and I said to him, 'What's the difference between eight hundred thousand dollars a year and a million three? What's the real difference at that level?' And he replied, 'Five hundred thousand dollars,' A great line. Wouldn't you agree?"

38. Gloria grew up in a less-than-financially-secure home. Her parents barely made ends meet. She earned money for college by working part-time for a well-known accounting firm. Gloria worked diligently for the money she made. One of the firm's power people took a liking to Gloria, and upon her graduation asked her to join the full-time staff. The job was great. The starting salary was certainly generous and the benefits were more than Gloria could have hoped for. Best of all, Gloria was assigned to her personal benefactor, who took her under his wing, taught her the ropes and became her "parent" in the company "family."

All that was a few years ago. Now, because of a recent merger there are changes in management philosophy and a change in Gloria's duties. Intellectually, Gloria knows it's time to move on, but feels guilty about looking elsewhere. She clearly recalls when she had close to nothing and the boss gave her a chance.

Which of the following advice would you offer to Gloria?

   a. "Gloria, you're a good, caring person. I commend you for your sense of loyalty. And you're probably right. Don't look elsewhere. Your boss probably needs you now more than ever, especially with the recent merger. Surely you agree you owe him a lot, and now's the time to repay your debt."

   b. "Gloria, you're a good, caring person. I commend you for your sense of loyalty. But you're wrong. If you feel you should look around for another opportunity, do so. The company hired you because you're good at what you do. Surely you've paid them back for their initial generosity by doing a good job, and your efforts have contributed to their bottom line. You've earned your salary, perks, and bonuses. And you've earned the right to look out for number one."

39. Many large companies have a policy that favors current employees when seeking to fill a higher-level or newly created position. Although they may prefer to promote from within, it is not always possible. The right person with the appropriate talents is not always on the company roster, so companies can be forced to recruit from outside the organization.

Perhaps you were selected from outside your current company, and you certainly will be coming in from the outside if you ultimately decide to leave your present organization. You might secure a job and find that a popular veteran worker there had competed for your job. This insider and his or her colleagues could be gunning for you. You could be denied the support you need from them when you get on the job.

If you were to find yourself in a situation where you would have to work with or supervise former rivals, do you honestly feel you'd have the political diplomacy to handle the situation? Can you convert a former adversary into a teammate?

   a. yes
   b. no

Ike Pappas, who was a television and radio journalist for CBS News for twenty-three years, now runs Ike Pappas Network Productions. He spoke about the difficulty in leaving CBS.

"I had thought for quite a while of leaving CBS because after twenty years at one place . . . 'What else is there?' The choice to leave was mine; the execution was CBS's. I thank them.

"You'd think when you get to the latter part of your life, after you've passed the age of fifty, you want security and a steady job. You don't want to run around a lot, you want to enjoy life, get extra time off. Well, I've never wanted that. I wanted to go on and see what else was out there. I wanted to leave but how could I do that without hurting a lot of people? I couldn't just quit. But I wanted to. It was frustrating. I just kept on doing my work, mechanically.

"The solution came when CBS laid off two hundred and fifteen people. I was one of the fortunate ones. They had to pay my entire salary for the next fifteen months. After that, I got a severance pay of over $200 thousand in a lump sum. I would then be eligible for early retirement and they would pay all my medical and dental expenses for the rest of my life. Just think, I get money just to get up in the morning!"

---

40. Matthew, age 48, gets good performance evaluations. However, some of his peers are always rated better and now five of them have been given promotions.

Matthew has read "the handwriting on the wall" and feels he has gone as far as he can go at his present company. He's considering a move to another company. Perhaps his chances for promotion will improve there.

When Matthew discusses this option with his wife, she feels it would be better if he stayed where he was.

What's your advice?

a. stay
b. leave

41. At a recent seminar, one of the participants approached us and remarked, "The people I work with are very clever, knowledgeable, and hard working, and most had good experience in other companies before they got here. While I'm holding my own in comparison, it's impossible for me to really stand out from the competition. Quite soon, there will be a few promotions offered. If I don't get one, should I stay there or leave?"

What advice would you give her?

a. "Stay put. You sound happy with your job. And more importantly, it sounds as if you have an opportunity to learn from your coworkers. Simply put, it's better to be an average fish in a selective pond than a big fish in muddy waters."

b. "Time to leave. You say you are a very capable person who can keep up with the best. If this company doesn't recognize your abilities, then you'd be better off in another company where there might be less competition. Simply put, it feels great to be a big fish, even in a smaller pond."

42. Select *one* of the following three sets of characteristics to best describe your boss.

Set A	Set B	Set C
accurate	confident	flexible
careful	decisive	optimistic
cautious	commanding	persuasive
orderly	innovative	helpful
says, "Let's check it out before we decide the next step."	says, "Let's go for it."	says, "Let's find out how others feel about it."

My boss is most like _____ (A, B or C).

Now select the *one* of the following sets that best describes those values that motivate you to do your best.

Set D	Set E	Set F
a variety of job tasks	job security	frequent challenges
freedom to make my own schedule	fairness	recognition for a job well done
frequent words of appreciation	not being taken for granted	to be held in high regard

I am most motivated by _____ (D, E or F).

Now combine your boss's set of characteristics and your set. Mark the appropriate choice on your answer sheet.

a. combinations A & E, B & F, or C & D
b. combinations A & D, B & D, C & E or C & F
c. combinations A & F or B & E

Actor, operatic tenor, author, sometime painter and sculptor, Paul Sorvino has appeared in more than twenty-five films, among them Reds, Bloodbrothers, *and* Oh God. *On stage he won the New York Drama Critics Circle Award and a Tony nomination for best actor, in the Pulitzer Prize–winning* That Championship Season. *He has recorded two Broadway show albums,* The Baker's Wife *and* Carmelina. *And he is the author of the best seller* How to Become a Former Asthmatic.

"When I was twenty-eight years old, newly married with a young child, I was acting but not making a living. A friend taught me how to write ad copy. I learned that once you're in the writing business, by definition you have a brain. To me, writing is instant proof of a complicated thought process. Just as a doctor wears a white coat, makes rounds and hears 'Good morning, Doctor,' I needed the 'Oh, he's a writer' thing. The uniform: the validation of my intellectual credentials. Interestingly enough, it was the first thing I was really successful at.

"As an actor I was much too difficult to cast because of my 'look.' In my twenties I had the physique of a gymnast and the face of a seventeen-year-old boy. Good for Li'l Abner but not much else. Money has never meant much to me, never entered into important negotiations with myself. I live well. I'm putting the kids through school, etc., etc.

"After six months as a junior writer, I became a very successful ad executive: Senior Vice-President, Creative Director. I had earned the uniform, the badge and title, name on the door, looming stock options and all the rest. But I decided to leave. Writing ad copy was not art; it was being an artist working for money at a 'job-job.' I was doing something I didn't want to be doing. I have so many ideas rolling around in my head that I must give full expression, feeling, and sensibility, ultimately binding them together with an artistic vision. Writing ad copy made me feel like a gourmet chef making bologna sandwiches.

"My wife encouraged me to go back into acting, where I could exercise some autonomy, be the artist I wanted to be. But I wondered, 'If I didn't make it before, why now?' Well, for one thing, I was two years older. The stress of marriage had caused me to add fifty pounds. I look different; character-actorish. I was coming out of a successful career. Why not now? Indeed. Besides, those 'intellectual credentials' were established. I bolted from the ad world and was a successful actor right from the start.

"I was then and am now seeking to fulfill myself in artistic ways. A certain destiny I feel compelled to live out. I wanted to be an actor from the time I was a child. At ten I developed a singing voice and began to dream of becoming an opera singer. That's where I'm headed now. Another tremendous career change.

"Stay or leave . . . I'm leaving again."

George F. Will came to Washington, D.C., as a congressional aide to Colorado senator Gordon Allott. In 1972 he became the Washington editor of The National Review. *His newspaper column has been syndicated since 1974 and now appears in more than 460 newspapers. He is also a television news analyst for the ABC–Capital Cities network. In 1981 he became a founding member of the panel of ABC's "This Week with David Brinkley."*

It was not his Federal style (1810) red-brick house on a quiet street in Georgetown or his second-floor office furnished in the same period that impressed Linda, but the man himself: George F. Will is a class act. He has the ability to give a class performance. During the interview, he impressed her with his ability to focus his thoughts until he found exactly the right position. No compromise.

Interview
George F. Will
Writer, news
analyst and
syndicated
newspaper
columnist

"I thought three years was enough working on the Senate staff of Gordon Allott of Colorado, since I wasn't going to make a career on Capitol Hill. So I planned to leave whether he won or lost the '72 election.

"I had written for some conservative publications, *The National Review* and *The Alternative,* and I called Bill Buckley and said I thought he needed a Washington editor. The person who headed the book section was, unfortunately, dying of cancer. So I had that career move in place when it was time to leave Senator Allott.

"I was probably a fair writer. I'm much better now. Anyone who does something for eighteen years has to get better at it. I've always enjoyed writing for quick pleasure. And still do. I don't think I knew at that point how satisfying writing could be. I plan to write forever. It is great catharsis. When I first starting writing, I asked Bill Buckley if he ever found it difficult trouble to write three columns, three times a week. 'No,' he said, 'the world irritates me that often.'

"The world—I would not say 'irritates' me . . . the world interests me at least that often. I would explode if I couldn't write. That's just a natural release like a steam valve.

"I like the solitary life; I can't bear meetings. Physically, I can't bear them . . . they make me ill. I'm just sick of meetings—they're a huge waste of time. They interfere with my work. My work is inherently solitary. I know committees have to exist in governments, collective and corporate enterprises. I understand the need. I just don't want to be part of it.

"This is right for me!"

43. Currently, a large number of baby boomers (now aged 35 to 45) have reached a comfortable level in middle management. For a variety of reasons (many upper-management people staying on the job well into their seventies; lack of expansion of their company or industry; increased competition for fewer opportunities; etc.), many boomers realize they may not go much higher.

What's your initial response if your baby-boomer friend says she's probably gone about as far as she can go?

    a. "All in all, you've got it pretty good. There's nothing wrong with staying at your job another fifteen years."

    b. "You should use your excess ability and energy to further your relationships with your family and improve the general quality of your life."

    c. "Why not start a part-time business on weekends and evenings? That way you'll have the security of your job plus new growth experiences."

    d. "It's simple. If there are no more steps to climb, get off this ladder and get on another that has more potential. Pack your traveling bag."

44. Imagine you're on your way to a new job and have agreed to interview the candidates for your current position before you go.

What three personal characteristics do you deem most important for the future success of your replacement?

1. _____

2. _____

3. _____

How many of the three above do you possess?

    a. all three

    b. two

    c. one

    d. none

Previous mistakes we have made, although thought dead and buried, sometimes have a way of rising again to haunt us. Take a moment to think back to the time you entered your current career path, and then answer questions 45 through 47.

45. Did you end up in an occupational field that your parents/friends/relatives pushed upon you ... a field you wouldn't have otherwise chosen on your own?

    a. yes
    b. no

46. Did you select your career path because it seemed to make the most use of your formal education ... even though you suspected it didn't fit your personality, values and interests?

    a. yes
    b. no

47. Did you jump into this field because you heard through radio, TV, newspapers and magazines, that opportunities would be plentiful ... without considering whether this field satisfied your personal needs?

    a. yes
    b. no

48. Most tasks you do at work make use of your abilities.

    a. true
    b. false

Company/Rewards Test

1. Most good companies, those with growth on their mind, usually have projects percolating. Core projects to streamline production, increase marketability, and enhance new product or service development are often among those given top priority. And there are less vital projects, too. Those commonly believed to have less of an effect upon the bottom line include redecorating the offices, planning the summer picnic and selecting a nutritionist for the company cafeteria.

    In the past two years, have you been asked to participate in company projects?

    a. yes
    b. no

2. Are you invited (selected or appointed) to join the more vital projects or committees?

    a. usually, yes
    b. occasionally
    c. rarely, if ever

3. Advancement in many organizations is based upon three attributes: personal influence, seniority and personal merit. But these qualities are not usually looked upon equally.

    Which of the six groupings below best typifies the way your company prioritizes these attributes?

A	B	C
1. influence	1. influence	1. seniority
2. seniority	2. merit	2. merit
3. merit	3. seniority	3. influence

D	E	F
1. seniority	1. merit	1. merit
2. influence	2. seniority	2. influence
3. merit	3. influence	3. seniority

Your company's ranking is group _____ (A, B, C, D, E, F).

Take a few moments and engage in some introspection. Which prioritized group is most similar to what you have to offer? _____

Are the two groups the same?

    a. yes
    b. no

4. If you deliberately asked your current employer to assign you to some alternative work functions outside of your present area of responsibility, do you think your request would be granted?

    a. yes
    b. no

5. How would you feel if you had to continue working in your present company (your job might change) for the rest of your working life?

    a. Fine. It's a good place to work.
    b. Okay. But I'm keeping my eyes and ears open for other positions within the company.
    c. Terrible. This is not the place for me.

6. One way a company can demonstrate its concern about your professional growth is to discuss your career goals and chances of promotion with you. When was the last time this happened?

    a. within the past twelve months
    b. within the past two years
    c. when I first interviewed for the position

7. Does your company have an organized mentoring program for which you are eligible?

    a. yes
    b. no

8. Have you taken advantage of a mentoring program if there is one, or have you approached more-senior executives who could serve as your mentor?

    a. yes
    b. no

9. There are companies that truly value new ideas suggested by employees; in other companies, people just nod their heads and make some empty gesture in response to proposed worthy innovations.

    Which of the two following statements more clearly defines your company's attitude toward new ideas?

    a. My company frequently gives money and assigns personnel to pursue innovative ideas, products or services.
    b. My company gives token gestures of interest in new ideas, products or services, then forms a study committee that tediously talks the idea to death.

Dr. Joyce Brothers is an author, columnist and business consultant, as well as an NBC Radio Network personality.

What influence can one petite, very feminine blonde psychologist have on the American public? A great deal, if the woman happens to be Dr. Brothers. She believes that in the long run "Money is secondary to personal challenge on-the-job . . . when you're confronted with a stay or leave decision."

"Many many years ago (back in 1955), after I won the $64,000 question, the International Boxing Club hired me to be a goodwill ambassador for the industry. I had no idea what to do. I went bananas. Finally, after two weeks, I couldn't take it anymore. So I went to the head of the organization and said 'You're all very nice people; I wish I could remain, but there's nothing for me to do, and I have never seen hours take so long in my life. Thank you very much. I'm returning the salary you paid me. Let's just remain friends.' "

10. If you had extra cash lying around, and stock in your company were available would you buy any?

    a. yes
    b. no

11. It has been going on for some time now. Your company has been downsizing. There haven't been mass firings—the decrease in personnel has come mainly through attrition. Obviously, more work has fallen on the shoulders of those who have stayed. You hear coworkers (high-level managers, peers and subordinates) say, "Damn it, now they want me to handle that, too" or, "They're taking advantage of me—I'm leaving."

    How do you perceive this situation?

    a. Chaos.
    b. Opportunity.

12. To the best of your knowledge, your company is operating on a fairly sound financial basis. You know of nothing impending that would cause a drastic change in the company's current goals or financial status.

    a. true
    b. false

According to Gary Edwards, Executive Director of the Ethics Resource Center, in Washington, D.C.:

"Sometimes, unrealistic goals are set by top management and good people feel extraordinary pressure to reach these profit/performance objectives. But reality doesn't always cooperate. What happens in most large organizations is a message gets sent that nobody intends to send . . . 'We don't care how you get there!'

"So as performance evaluations are done, managers go by the numbers and they know you *got* there, but *not* how. And most of the time the boss doesn't seem to care.

"The young and ambitious want to be CEOs some day so they can't fail to meet those objectives early in their careers. Others have two kids in college and a mortgage and they can't afford to lose their jobs. And so some wind up doing things they're ashamed of, compromising their personal integrity and morality, often violating the law and all the time justifying it to themselves—by saying they're doing it for the company.

"I made a decision to leave a small company where I was manager of a distribution center and reported directly to the vice-president. The president and executive vice-president were substantial equity holders. My immediate boss had no equity in the company and worked very hard as a key person. He apparently made a judgment that he was inadequately compensated, or otherwise not treated right, because he took some of the products slated for distribution, and marked them out of inventory as damaged. My boss then set up a dummy company and sold these products for substantial discounts to our other customers.

"I found myself in a rather difficult position where the only people I could tell about his activities were the principals of the firm. And because I understood my boss's place in the hierarchy, I thought it was very unlikely that he was going to be fired.

"So I prepared my letter of resignation along with photocopies of the dummy invoices and falsified inventory records. I took them to New York and turned them over to the president of the company and told him that the company had an obligation to its clients to make restitution and that it seemed likely that there had been some laws broken, mail fraud perhaps, and that there was a lot that had to be set right. I told him that I didn't expect them to fire the vice president and I wasn't willing to work for him any longer, so I left.

"That was a hard job to leave, because I didn't have another. There was no safety net."

13. Rich, a 27-year-old salesman who worked for a small clothing firm, was offered a position in a prestigious designer's company. His new starting salary was comparable to the old one, his title was not embellished and the tasks he had to do were similar. We asked Rich why he made the move.

"I'm counting on this company's reputation. Everyone in the industry knows it. I think it's better to work for a company with a high visibility that a little-known one. I'll be rubbing shoulders with the top people."

What about you? Would you switch companies to work for one with a more prestigious reputation?

    a. yes
    b. no

14. If you're working in a family-run business, and are not part of the clan, you'd be wise to realize that most likely you'll not reach the very top slots. They're reserved for family members whether they're qualified or not.

Select the one that *best* pertains to you.

    a. I do not work in a family-run business.
    b. I work in a family-run business and I'm part of the clan.
    c. I work in a family-run business. I'm not part of the clan and do not wish to rise to the top. I like what I do.
    d. I work in a family-run business and I'm not part of the clan. The senior members promised me a quick rise to the top. That was more than two years ago and little has happened since.

15. Certain large companies have a reputation for frequently buying and selling divisions. There is nothing wrong with this from the company's perspective; just like employees, if they remain stagnant they may wither.

However, if you are in middle management or above, a possible takeover or sell-off makes your position vulnerable. Quite often, a new management team is brought in by the new parent company.

Based upon your present knowledge (annual reports, office grapevine, competitor's chitchat, etc.) is your department or division a possible takeover or sell-off candidate?

    a. Yes, and I'm in middle management or above.
    b. No.
    c. Yes, and I'm in a clerical or support-staff position.

16. Based on the information available to you (sales invoices, number of new clients, annual report, increase in number of employees) your company is _____.

    a. growing
    b. stagnating
    c. slipping in stature

The King of Nostalgia sat on a rickety chair and held court in the midst of his mountain of stuff in his ten-by-twenty-foot midtown New York office not far from Times Square. The picture was priceless and Linda fondly recalls the visit with Joe Franklin, America's longest-running television host and owner of Joe Franklin Productions, when she sat on a wobbly stool between two constantly ringing phones.

Mr. Franklin's Stay or Leave story is about one of the few times in his life he hesitated before taking action. He usually works with authority. He makes fast decisions. But there was one time when he pondered leaving a job where he was making no money for a job that could possibly make double nothing—or perhaps fifteen or thirty dollars a week. He was glad he left.

"When I was about seventeen years old I was written up in a magazine as being a young collector of old nostalgia records. I had thousands of old records in my collection. And I got a phone call from local radio station WHOM on West 57th Street. They had read the article and offered me the chance to be an emcee of my own records one night a week. I went down and made a deal with them to host a program called 'Vaudeville Echoes.'

"It was scheduled every Saturday night for thirty minutes. And when it came time to go on the air I asked them about salary. They said, 'no salary,' but it would give me 'good exposure.' So I did the show for four weeks, no money, but I really loved it. And then I got a phone call, this time from WNEW, a major station, number one in the ratings. They had a program called 'Make Believe Ballroom' with Martin Block and they asked me if I would consider switching my program to WNEW. It was a very big decision because I was very happy where I was.

"I asked them what I would get paid. They answered, 'whatever you're getting paid now, we'll give you double.' I had to think fast. This was what you would call 'being in a pinch,' a crisis moment. I said to myself because I was very young and naive, and inexperienced . . . 'If I ask for too much I'll probably blow it, if I tell them the truth, they'll have no respect for me.' So what I did, I said, 'I'm now making fifteen dollars a week,' 'Joe,' they said 'we'll give you thirty.' I thought it over, talked to my parents, my friends, and reluctantly left the station where I was very comfortable. At WNEW I started at thirty dollars a week, making fourteen times thirty, plus I was chosen to select the records for Martin Block, which I thought was a big honor. I was glad I made that decision to leave because from then on my salary went up."

17. A certain degree of on-the-job boredom is to be expected in any profession, from abstractor to zoologist. No job is fascinating every minute of every day. But before you don your job-seeking outfit, there are two things you may want to try.

If you have a good working relationship with your boss, ask for an extra performance review. Ask: "What things do I do well and in what areas can I improve?" The answers to this double-barreled question can give you something extra to work toward and may relieve on-the-job-boredom.

Have you had this type of discussion lately?

    a.   No.
    b.   Yes, and I'm still bored.

18. Sometimes on-the-job boredom takes its toll because we don't expand our circle of friends within the company. We see the same people, the ones who work near us, day after day. Have you cultivated friends outside your inner working circle or department?

    a.   No.
    b.   Yes, and I'm still bored.

19. Taking a position with a company that is downsizing can be quite risky. Your new job could be on next month's elimination list. But layoffs can create some unusually interesting opportunities if you happen to be at the right place at the right time. After initial layoffs, companies frequently announce their new goals and begin to grow anew.

How much of a risk-taker are you?

    a.   I would not seriously consider a job with a company currently laying off employees.
    b.   If the job sounded right for me, sure I'd take the chance.

20. Does your company . . .

    a.   prepare for continuity of leadership? Cultivate young men and women to take over top management positions?
    b.   solely rely on the *creative geniuses* who started the business? Are they failing to provide eventual succession?

21. Which reaction do you have to the following statement? Before I can move on to a more responsible position, I really need to know my present job more thoroughly.

    a.   agree
    b.   disagree
    c.   no opinion

22. You foresee your immediate supervisor's position as your next step for advancement. It makes sense you should . . .

    a. slip small, daily doses of arsenic into her coffee.

    b. do all that you can to assist her advancement.

    c. let everyone know that your boss is incompetent.

23. Jason has been at the same position in the same company for three years. He has done his job well, but has become totally bored by it. He's reached the point that if he continues doing the same thing any longer, he feels he will go out of his mind. There's no upward slot available now or in the foreseeable future.

    Jason discussed his dilemma with his boss, who made him this offer: "Would you accept a change in position even if it's considered a demotion? Your daily work pattern would change and I'd make sure your salary remains stable."

    If you were Jason, what would you do?

    a. Stay put and let the chips fall where they may.

    b. Take the boss's offer; anything is better than the current situation.

24. Does your company invest in training and development programs at nearly all employee levels?

    a. yes

    b. no

Interview
Robert Gray
Editor of Nation's
Business

Robert Gray, Editor of Nation's Business, *came to this magazine as a political/legislative analyst. In forty years, he has made only two job changes. He had worked for a small newspaper, and with the natural progression of things, Mr. Gray got bored. He decided it was time to work for a larger organization, and became a correspondent for the Associated Press.*

"I became bored because the work became repetitious. Some people like that. It's their sense of security, a feeling that everything that comes up can be handled. But in those situations, there's no growth. I was a political/governmental writer and was looking for a larger playing field, in the big leagues.

    "When I made the switch, I was a rookie in a new field. I had to learn who the players were, make new business contacts and establish relationships with the new people I was working with.

    "When switching, you must be patient because it takes time to know everyone and time to get to know the issues."

Peter D. Hart, Chairman and Chief Executive Officer of Peter D. Hart Research Associates, is one of the leading analysts of public opinion surveys. As one of the top Democratic political analysts, he has aided Senate leaders such as Hubert Humphrey, Lloyd Bentsen, Edward Kennedy and Bill Bradley. He recently told us of his decision to become actively involved in politics:

"I was working as an analyst at Louis Harris in New York, January, 1968. I had the best position one could have on the creative side of a survey-research firm.

"In the world around me there was Vietnam going on. There was the election challenge to Lyndon Johnson, and a sense that 1968 was going to be a very dramatic year. As I sat there on the top floor of the old Henry Luce Suite overlooking the skaters in Rockefeller Center I said to myself, 'This is crazy, this isn't what it's all about. I don't care if any company sells ten or a thousand or gives away a thousand more securities. That's not what counts. What counts is what's happening out there in the world.' I decided to leave and put my energies instead into politics.

"It's important to me that I be where history is being made. I didn't want to be on the outside casually looking at it. I wanted to be involved. I had no sense where it was going to lead me nor any sense of money being important. Money wasn't what it was really about.

"Out there I learned that I had a whole bunch of skills I didn't know I had. The ability to organize, motivate, to understand—is the difference it takes to make it in politics. Most importantly, I learned what politics is all about—the personal relationships, animosities and intricacies of the political world. While learning that, you learn a lot about yourself."

25. How many of the following pertain to your current job situation?

- There's no opportunity for equity participation.
- Your industry is becoming obsolete.
- Your company's most prevailing leadership style is weak and indecisive.
- Nearly all of your assignments are unchallenging.

    a. four
    b. three
    c. two
    d. one
    e. none

26. During the past few years, the turnover rate among the senior staff has risen sharply.

    a. true
    b. false

27. Are you good at your job, yet hate it?

    a. yes
    b. no

28. Frequently, it's not possible to step out of the job you have directly into the job you want. Sometimes the change requires two steps . . . you may have to take a transitional job for a year or so.

    Are you willing to put up with double the hassles to get where you want to go?

    a. yes
    b. no

29. Do you have a clear idea of what that transitional job might be?

    a. yes
    b. no

When in the market for another job, people are usually attempting to get away from a perceived negative situation or trying to enhance their current position by moving up in power, money, prestige, etc. Most people experience both types of moves during their career.

Moving up often leads to increased supervisory responsibilities and one of the most difficult managerial functions to master is the art of effective delegation . . . a key to managerial success.

In questions 30 through 35, let's see if you're ready to leave and move up. React to the following statements.

30. Delegation relieves the manager/supervisor from routine and noncritical tasks.

    a. strongly agree
    b. agree
    c. disagree
    d. strongly disagree

31. You should realize that when you delegate the job it will not be done as well as you could have done it.

    a. strongly agree
    b. agree
    c. disagree
    d. strongly disagree

32. You've delegated a task and your subordinate later lets you know he or she cannot quite figure out how to do it. To save time and avoid the employee embarrassment you respond, "Here, let me do it."

    a. strongly agree
    b. agree
    c. disagree
    d. strongly disagree

33. You cannot delegate everything. There are things that must be done by you alone.

    a. strongly agree
    b. agree
    c. disagree
    d. strongly disagree

34. After you have fully explained the delegated task, you should ask your subordinate to tell you in his or her own words what he or she understands the assignment to be.

    a. strongly agree
    b. agree
    c. disagree
    d. strongly disagree

35. If your employee fails to do the delegated task effectively, he or she, not you, will be in real hot water with upper management. It's a well-known fact, when you delegate responsibilities you also delegate the accountability for them.

    a. strongly agree
    b. agree
    c. disagree
    d. strongly disagree

36. Promotions should be awarded to those who _____.

    a. work hard and perform well on the job
    b. are diligent and pay attention to the details of their present position
    c. aren't afraid to challenge coworkers (or the boss).
    d. can demonstrate they have the skills for the next level

In February 1989, Judith Richards Hope, a senior litigation partner with Paul, Hastings, Janofsky & Walker, was the first woman elected to serve on Harvard University's highest governing board, the Harvard Corporation. When Linda spoke to her in 1988, Ms. Hope had just been nominated by President Reagan to fill Judge Robert Bork's vacated seat on the U.S. Court of Appeals for the District of Columbia Circuit. While she was declining all substantive press interviews on her nomination, she was willing to talk about her views on making such a significant career decision.

"This was one of the toughest decisions I have ever made. My law firm is my intellectual home. What's more, I am doing what I love; litigation and trial practice, with a few arguments in the Court of Appeals as well. The people I work with here are not only my colleagues but also my friends. And necessarily, when you go on the bench, you must close yourself off from all of those who have cases before you—the very people I work with so closely now. In addition, I have just been elected as the first woman director of the Union Pacific Corporation, headquartered in Bethlehem, Pennsylvania. Being elected a director of a Fortune 500 company is both a great honor and a real opportunity to serve. Yet, on balance, the opportunity to be of service to the country was so great that I felt I could not turn down the President's nomination.

"In addition, I know that I have made a number of career changes during my professional life and, looking back, they have all proved to be for the better. In 1975, for example, my husband and I were called from California to Washington to work in the Ford administration. Even though we were happy and well settled in a beautiful new home outside

37. It wasn't too long ago that your company selected you to be a part of a newly organized program it was enthusiastic about. Now, it seems, "that was then"; today, your gut says this program is no longer on your company's priority list.

    Have you, or others in your company, had this experience lately?

    a. yes
    b. no

38. In your present company, most employees . . .

    a. understand their role, functions and obligations.
    b. feel confused about their role, functions and obligations.

Los Angeles, both of us had and have a strong commitment to public service and we felt we could not turn President Ford down. The job I was asked to fill was in a completely new area for me: Associate Director of the White House Domestic Council, focusing on transportation policy. I had to learn a whole new area of the law, to understand how it was changing (it was the beginning of transportation deregulation, and I was to be the White House coordinator of that massive change), and also to understand what the administration's policies should be and how they should be coordinated and implemented. I learned. And fast! In the process I discovered that I was a pretty good administrator. I found that I was able to work with a large number of people involved with both policies and politics. And, at the end of each day, I felt that I had made a tiny contribution to perhaps making the world and this country a little bit better place. The pay cut I took to enter government was insignificant in comparison with the chance President Ford gave me to try to accomplish something important in this country.

"It was an exciting time. But, when it was over, I was eager to return to the thing that I loved the most—practicing law and trying cases. The courtroom is one of the few places where our system and our freedoms are on the line every day. With winning or losing at stake, it is 'content living' at the highest level, as my mentor and first employer, the late Edward Bennett Williams, always said. Having been in the advocate's role in the courtroom for the better part of a quarter of a century, I feel that if I am confirmed as a judge it will be a new and exciting challenge to shed the advocate's role for that of the impartial decision-maker. And once again, I may have the chance to try to make the world just a little bit better if I can do my job right."

39. The word in your industry is that competing companies have little respect for yours.

    a. true
    b. false

40. Many companies tend to be overly optimistic and expand too much at the top of a business cycle. Then, when a financial downturn comes, they have a particularly rough time.

    Would you say your company has followed this pattern?

    a. yes
    b. no

Mike Nevard is Associate Publisher and Editorial Director of Globe Communications Corp., publishers of weekly tabloids and magazines. At the age of twenty Mr. Nevard moved to London and joined the jazz weekly Melody Maker. *Within five years he had become its Deputy Editor. Since then, it's clear he's followed a general rule: "If something appears to be a step up—take it."*

"I virtually ran the paper and became recognized internationally as a jazz authority. And then one day I was approached out of the blue by the *Daily Herald,* which was owned by the same company. Again, I had to make a decision to stay or leave. It would mean going into a much broader field. I would be going from being a big fish in a fairly big pond to a very small fish in a bigger pond. Once more I decided I should leave to broaden my life. I stayed with the *Herald* for fifteen years, but the paper wasn't doing very well. Rupert Murdoch bought the company and I had to decide whether to stay with the umbrella company, which offered me a job as publisher of a garden magazine just because I had moved to a house in the country and had a garden, or to go with this powerful buccaneer. I'd heard all kinds of stories about him. I decided to take a chance with Rupert Murdoch. Only a few of us went out of hundreds.

"It was very exciting working for Rupert Murdoch. I learned more in the five years at his *Sun* than anywhere, because I was part of a creative team and could do virtually whatever I wanted to do. And what I was producing was what I liked to produce. I was very much geared towards the audience we wanted to reach. I felt at ease and excited. It was very stimulating. I worked seven days a week when we first started.

"I was running the features for the *Sun,* and was one of the creative team of five people. You could say I was one of Rupert's commandoes. He wanted to go to the United States to take on the *National Enquirer* and for me to help set it up, and find an American staff. That was fifteen years ago. It was a big decision to make at forty-five. It meant starting a new life in a new country. I decided to leave. It was the year my daughter had won a scholarship to Oxford; my wife was very happy where she was. Without her, I would never had made it. She supported me in every career move I made. But she felt I put my career first before my family, which in fact is quite true. I thought America would be exciting and challenging. It didn't take too long before I discovered I was not very happy with the situation I found myself in—I felt I was getting used. I thought as Managing Editor I was producing the *Star,* and when Rupert Murdoch made one appointment of an Australian as editor, I told him I was very unhappy about it.

"A year later, I was approached by the *National Enquirer* to be number two—again as Managing Editor. That was a very big jump for me because ever since I'd been in London I had been taken over or moved from one publication to another in the same group. I had never actually jumped ship as it were. This was a big step. Again, I decided to leave for more opportunity.

"I soon found at the *Enquirer* you have to fit the mold—there's not much room for creativity. You have to do things the way Eneroso Pope wants them done. He comes from the Massachusetts Institute of Technology and he runs the paper like an engineer. It's very much his paper. He's involved in everything. There just wasn't room for my creative talents. I was there for six months and I had to make a very quick decision to stay or leave. We had a conversation one day when he told me that I had to do things his way and I said, 'I think I made a mistake, and you made a mistake, in my coming here.' And he said, 'I think you're right.' And that was it. It was over in about five minutes.

"That same evening I got a phone call from Rupert Murdoch. 'You can come to me for an editorship in Australia, New York, London, wherever you want to be,' he said. At that point, I had enough money to sit back for a while. I had to really decide what I wanted to do. I decided to take a job as an assistant editor at Rupert's *New York Post*. Rupert is a very persuasive man. And when you work for him you work hard. I was working long hours again, but enjoying it. I even got back to do some jazz writing, which was fun. I had been at the *Post* for only a month when Bill Davis, who was chairman of New York Times Magazines, asked me to be editor of *US* magazine, and I said 'No, I've come back to Rupert and I'm not going to leave again.'

"Soon after this offer, I was told that if I went to a certain hotel in New York and met someone I would get a sensational book series for the *New York Post*. So when I finished about 9:00 that night I went to the hotel and found there was no book series. The person I was to meet turned out to be Mike Rosenbloom, who owns Globe Communications, which was publishing at that time *Midnight Globe,* the *National Examiner* and a string of magazines from Montreal. He wanted me to be editorial director of the group. Again, a very big decision, because I was working with Rupert, and I was very happy. However, I reasoned that I left England to come to America to create a tabloid in America—a weekly paper. And that's what I really wanted to do. And once again, the challenge excited me. So I left Rupert.

"I eventually became Associate Publisher and a vice-president of the company, and moved our operations to Florida. I have been with *Globe* now for nine years. I feel this is where I should be . . . every day is different, every story is different."

Stephen Schlossberg has been Director of the Washington branch of the International Labor Office and Special Advisor to the Director-General of the I.L.O. since September 1987. He spoke of an early job in retailing. He was quite good in the position because he had an eye for advertising, style and color. But Schlossberg's interests were not attuned to what he was doing:

"What I was concerned about was right there in the same city. People were being victimized and taken advantage of in factories, in stores and everywhere else. Black people were denied basic human rights because of the color of their skin. So, my natural allies became in a political sense, the black civil-rights movement, the intellectuals and the few bohemians who were the writers, the artists and the trade union people who lived here. They were expressing some of the concerns that the Old Testament's prophets had: social justice, individual dignity, the inhumanity of man to man and the necessity of standing up to that.

"In that light, it became incredibly difficult for me to go to work every day and tell some lady she looked great in a dress when it only may have mattered to her husband and maybe her lover. But it certainly didn't matter to me."

41. If you truly hunger for a fabulous Chinese dinner, starting with the delicious appetizer rumaki, continuing with the chef's special chicken along with a sumptuous order of ten-ingredient fried rice, and ending with fresh pineapple chunks and the all-important fortune cookie, you would not make reservations at an elegant Italian restaurant. That's quite obvious.

Yet some people make a far more serious error when they take a job and don't find out what possible rewards are being served. Different companies, departments, industries offer different rewards.

Here's a list of basic rewards for a job well done. Select the three currently most important to you and enter them in the spaces provided. Also, you may insert any rewards of importance that do not appear on the following list.

- Money
- A sense of accomplishment
- Prestige
- Freedom to experiment
- Company-paid retirement plans
- Power
- Travel
- Constant challenge

- An opportunity to grow professionally
- Generous vacation time
- Comprehensive health plans

1. _____

2. _____

3. _____

Now, the important question. Considering the three rewards you selected as "most important," would you say you are adequately rewarded in your present job?

a. yes
b. no

42. What's your perception?

a. At your level, your company usually promotes from within the organization.
b. At your level, your company usually looks to outsiders to fill new or vacant positions.
c. At your level, your company looks for the best people to fill new or vacant positions, whether they are current employees or not.

Stress Test

1. Which of the following best completes this sentence? The common minor frustrations of everyday life (the shoelace that breaks, the nasty weather, the missed telephone call, the tie or blouse that has a stain) _____.

   a. create a considerable inner tension and the beginning stages of your stress buildup.
   b. hit you for the moment, but not for long.
   c. have very little impact upon your behavior.

2. When the majority of people talk about their job-related stress, they usually mention pressures brought on by work overload, time constraints, threats from the boss or stressful social situations. But this is not always the case.

   Daphine works in a state agency that had experienced tremendous expansion in the past four years. About a year ago, the need for more employees diminished, but hiring continued at the accelerated pace. Now, according to Daphine, there are too many employees and there's not enough to do. Daphine says, "I'm experiencing stress, a stress of work underload."

   Grace works in an entry-level position in a St. Louis advertising agency. She's been there three years, and although she found the first year a definite learning experience, the time since then has been a drag because she's still doing basically the same tasks. Grace does her job well, but neither has the company expanded appreciably nor have positions become available through attrition. The opportunity to move up into a more challenging slot is not on the horizon. Does this sound familiar?

   Work underload, no matter what the reason, can cause stress for some people. How many of the following are you currently experiencing?

   - Not enough work to do.
   - A requirement to look busy although you're not.
   - Not enough responsibility.
   - Mind, skills and ability not used.
   - Overqualification for the job.
   - No chance for personal growth.

   a. all six
   b. five or four
   c. three or two
   d. one or none

3. On the average, how often do you take home psychological problems packed away in your work-stuffed briefcase?

      a. almost every day
      b. about every other day
      c. about once a week
      d. hardly ever

4. Through the years, we have discovered that only a handful of people readily admit they are totally satisfied with their job. The vast majority will, if given the opportunity and confidentiality, complain about one or more irritating aspects of their work. If frustration mounts and multiplies, their perception of the total job may deteriorate, and chances are they'll soon imagine everything to be far worse than it actually is.

    The following checklist is an overview. It's your opportunity to quickly compare your current situation with the most commonly mentioned stresses we've uncovered. Perhaps you'll discover that you're not as bad off as you think. And then again . . .

    For each of the following comments, designate whether it is currently present in or absent from your job.

	Present	Absent
Overload Situations		
"No matter what I do, the work is never done."	____	____
"I'm responsible for too many people."	____	____
"I must regularly take work home to finish it."	____	____
"My superiors impose unrealistic deadlines upon me."	____	____
Underload Situations		
"There's just not enough work to do."	____	____
"My mind, skills and abilities are not used."	____	____
"I have to invent ways to look busy."	____	____
"Putting it mildly, I'm overqualified for the job."	____	____
It's a Dead-End Job		
"There's no hope for advancement in the organization."	____	____
"I find definite evidence of sex, age and racial discrimination at work."	____	____
"I can't do what I do best."	____	____
"The work I do has little meaning to me."	____	____

Security

"There's a constant talk of possible layoffs."   ___ ___

"The health insurance plan is inadequate."   ___ ___

"I'm exposed to unhealthy working conditions."   ___ ___

"This job involves frequent physical danger and threats   ___ ___
of violence from others."

The Boss

"Simply put, my boss is incompetent."   ___ ___

"My boss has found his/her resting place. He/she has   ___ ___
retired on the job."

"Criticism, criticism. That's all I get."   ___ ___

"I don't have one boss, I have three!"   ___ ___

Time

"There's not sufficient time allowed for coffee breaks   ___ ___
or an adequate lunch."

"Rotating shifts may seem democratic, but they're   ___ ___
playing havoc with my personal life."

"Even if requested, there's no time given to conduct   ___ ___
personal affairs."

"Absolutely no flexibility in starting or quitting times."   ___ ___

Record the total number of "presents" and "absents."

Totals: ___ P ___ A

Subtract the smaller number from the larger. The result is _____.
Mark the appropriate choice on your answer sheet.

    a. 8P or more
    b. 2P to 6P
    c. 0 to 4A
    d. 6A or more

5.   Is this you? "Both on and off the job, one of my biggest mistakes is trying
to handle too many things at once. That dilutes my efforts and few things
come out as I hoped they would."

    a. That's me, more or less.
    b. No, that's not my problem.

6. Achieving men and women are increasingly becoming overwhelmed with all there is to get done. Workplace pressures, additional family responsibilities and, for some, inner psychological drives often create an inordinate amount of stress.

Sure, stress in proper doses can be worthwhile, for it may help muster up that extra effort needed to get things done. But there's a fine line that separates stress that motivates from self-destructive stress. Have you crossed over the line? For each of the following items, place a check mark in the appropriate column.

	Yes	No
• Compared to a year ago, are you now:		
smoking more cigarettes?	——	——
drinking more alcoholic beverages?	——	——
using more drugs?	——	——
• Compared to six months ago, are you:		
catching more frequent colds?	——	——
experiencing more intestinal or stomach pains?	——	——
suffering from more recurring headaches?	——	——
suffering from more recurring backaches?	——	——
ten pounds heavier (and not pregnant)?	——	——
• Within the past six months, have you:		
forgotten more appointments than usual?	——	——
missed more deadlines?	——	——
misplaced more personal belongings?	——	——
• Recently, has sex become an activity that's not worth the effort?	——	——
• You may need an extra moment to think about this. Do you find yourself more often talking about your personal problems than actually doing something to solve them?	——	——
• Lately, have you felt depressed, discouraged and generally down on yourself because you haven't reached your own high standards?	——	——
• Do you typically schedule more things each day than you can possibly get done?	——	——
• Have you noticed that others are avoiding you, professionally or personally?	——	——

Now, total the check marks in the "Yes" column. What's your "Yes" total? _____ Mark the appropriate choice on your answer sheet.

a. 0–4
b. 5–9
c. 10–14
d. 15–17

Questions 7 through 10 pertain to the following paragraph.

Believe it or not, one major and often overlooked reason for thinking about changing jobs is not having enough to do. The stress associated with work overload is obvious but the stress of work underload can be just as destructive.

7. Do you often feel there's not enough for you to do?

   a. yes
   b. no

8. Are you expected to look busy when you're not?

   a. yes
   b. no

9. Do you feel you're overqualified for your job?

   a. yes
   b. no

10. Do you feel there's not much chance for personal growth because there's just too little to do?

    a. yes
    b. no

11. *After* you read this first line, take three deep breaths. Now, close your eyes and relax for a moment or two. That's good. Imagine you are walking along a gorgeous tropical beach. Feel the warm sun on your back, smell the salty air, sense the soft sand under your feet. Now lie down on a towel you've placed on the smooth, white sand and listen to the quiet, rhythmic sound of the gentle waves. Stay with this relaxing mood for another moment or two.

    Now list the three most pressing problems you have with your present job. Keep in mind that you're still on that tropical beach. Can you imaginatively create solutions within your current situation to . . .

    a. all three job problems?
    b. two of the problems?
    c. one problem?
    d. none of them?

12. Many of us who work diligently also dream and fantasize about having more free time. That is, time with no deadlines, no telephone ringing, no messages, no commuting headaches, no decisions to make. Sound good? You bet it does. However, some who profess a desire for totally free time become emotionally uncomfortable once they finally find themselves with nothing to do.

   Let's say you and your spouse, lover or friend plan a two-week vacation to a tropical isle just to soak up the sun's rays and totally relax. Before the first week is over, you're getting fidgety—then irritable—and you find yourself returning before the two weeks have elapsed.

   Has this happened, or could this happen to you? Select the response that best describes you.

   a. "Not me at all! When I get away from work, I'm truly away from it all—literally and figuratively."
   b. "No, I've never actually returned early from a vacation, but I've been on the verge of doing so a number of times."
   c. "Yes. An emergency arose at work and it was necessary that I return."
   d. "Yes. Two weeks is a long time to be away from it all. When I'm on vacation, I call the office each day and if things get too hectic there, I must return."

13. "It's difficult to get away for any continuous length of time. So what I do is take long summer weekends by adding a Friday and/or Monday. But of course, I take paperwork with me."

   a. That's me to a T!
   b. That's me, more or less.
   c. That's not really me, but there are some similarities.
   d. That's not me at all!

14. "Vacations? Are you crazy? This place is so busy I can't afford to take time off. I've tried, but whenever I do, I start to feel guilty because I know the work is piling way up. In fact, recently I've had to come in on weekends just to catch up."

   a. That's me to a T!
   b. That's me, more or less.
   c. That's not really me, but there are some similarities.
   d. That's not me at all!

15. Nearly everyone, from time to time, brings work problems and anxieties home at the end of a day. That's quite natural. But do those problems frequently contaminate the quality of your personal life?

   Try this. In the spaces below quickly insert eight leisure activities that

Paul H. Alvarez, Chairman and Chief Executive Officer of Ketchum Public Relations, the seventh-largest public relations firm in the United States, says money is no longer his main goal.

"A year and a half ago, I had a very tempting offer to leave Ketchum and have my name on the door of another agency. It took a lot of time to make a decision and I weighed the pros and cons. I decided not to leave my present position as Chairman of Ketchum for that chance. I thought, after all, I had already proven my worth. I had always gotten more responsibilities and promotions at Ketchum. I decided I didn't want the pressures involved starting from scratch to prove myself all over again. Furthermore, I felt the agency in mind was stretching everything they had to make me feel comfortable. And this put pressure on me. I was flattered, of course, but on the other hand, I felt I couldn't disappoint them. I had to be letter-perfect and that made me feel uncomfortable."

you enjoy—for instance, playing tennis, fishing, reading a novel, going to the movies, whatever.

Eight Activities I Enjoy

1. _____   5. _____

2. _____   6. _____

3. _____   7. _____

4. _____   8. _____

Select one of the following.

a. I could not name eight leisure-time activities I enjoy.
b. I did name eight leisure-time activities I enjoy.

16. Now go back to question 15 and add to each item on your list the approximate date you last did it and enjoyed it. We'll wait for you here.

Review the dates you entered and determine how many of the eight leisure-time activities you participated in during the past four months.

a. all eight
b. four to seven of them
c. one to three
d. none of them

Jack Valenti, President and Chief Executive Officer of one of the most dazzling and mesmerizing arenas in the world, the Motion Picture Association of America, tells us a Stay or Leave story of a time in his life when his timing was exquisite and he didn't even know it.

"Sometimes you do things that in retrospect look very intelligent, and very wise, but have no roots in wisdom at all. It's just that you made a decision and think it's not going to be the best one. And it turns out that in the passage of time it was a congenial decision in the sense that it matched where life was going.

"When I got out of Harvard Business School I went back to Texas. And in two years I had organized my own advertising business. It was hard work, but the business was building, and doing very well.

"Meanwhile, about three years after I had cofounded the agency Weekley and Valenti I met the majority leader of the U.S. Senate, Lyndon B. Johnson. He would come to Texas, and in each city he would try to meet young people under thirty-five to replenish his 'Palace Guard,' which a lot of politicians fail to do. They age and their supporters age and they bring in nobody new. So he was constantly refreshing his campaign organization with new people.

"We met in 1955, and after that I volunteered to write speeches for him, and did some political volunteer work. And every time he came to Houston, I would be among those who would be asked to meet with the majority leader. He got to know me. And then in 1962, I married one of Johnson's chief lieutenants, Mary Margaret Wiley. He was fond of her, she was loyal to him, so I got to know him a lot better. In 1963, my agency had been in business about thirteen years. For the first time, I had a substantial income for those days, and we were on our way to becoming one of the biggest advertising agencies in Texas. We were well managed, our costs were kept down, our clients satisfied, and we were making money. Vice-President Johnson asked me to manage the press, and the trip to Houston, and then to get involved with the dinner in Austin the night of November 22. My agency wrote and printed the program for that event. The Vice-President said 'Things are going so well, you come with me to Fort Worth and Dallas, and let your people handle Austin. We'll fly to Austin together.' So I did.

"I was in the motorcade when Kennedy was assassinated. I was ordered to come aboard Airforce One by the new President. President

Johnson said to me when I arrived at Airforce One, 'I want you on my staff and you're going to fly back to Washington with me.'

"I had one night's clothes, no place to live ('You can live at the White House until your family comes up,' he said). At that moment there was really no decision to make because the President said, 'I want you on my staff!' And though I wasn't quite sure what that exactly meant, I accepted.

"When I got to Washington, he called me into his office and said, 'I want you to get rid of your business, and anything that would be a conflict of interest, and come on board with me.'

"I wasn't sure I wanted to do it. I had a wonderful life in Houston. I had my own business. I didn't have any board of directors over me. I wasn't reporting to anyone. I was building something that was, at least to my eyes, a vision that I was on an exciting adventure. I didn't quite understand then the historical role that one plays in the White House.

"And then when I asked the President what my salary would be he said, 'Let's find out.' He called the Chief Clerk, Bill Hopkins, and said, 'Bill, I want Jack put on my payroll at the highest salary I can pay him.' 'What is that?' I asked. He put the phone down and said, 'You're making $19,000 a year.' That was about one-fifth of what I was making. And in those days $19,000 wasn't starvation wages but it was a hell of a lot less than the $100,000 I was making in my business. So I was thunderstruck. But the thing that finally determined my decision was twofold. Number one, I didn't think that when the President of the United States asks you to do something you could turn it down, no matter what are the fiscal sacrifices you have to make. Then I began to realize this was a new turn in my life. I was going to be operating on the largest proscenium in the world. It would be historically relevant and daily challenging. I would be serving my country, which is the most exciting adventure of them all. I didn't realize it then but when you're right by the side of the President you take on the ambiance of power. It's a vicarious power, but nonetheless it's heady stuff. But I didn't know that at the time.

"It was a turn in my life that I had not planned on, and one I had misgivings about for a few weeks. I thought I was giving up so much but it turned out my life lifted to a new level. It went on from there catching hold of an outer edge of an ascending curve. Again, I wasn't sure where this curve was going to take me, what summit I would finally land on, or if I would land anywhere for that matter. But that's how it happened."

17. Some people feel the world owes them a decent job. They're partially correct. The world will offer them a job, but not always a quality one they would want to hang on to for very long.

Before you decide to make the Stay or Leave decision, you'll need to know the price you pay for indecision. The price, plus the high personal interest on that price, can last for numerous years.

How many of the following symptoms of indecision are you currently experiencing?

- Depression
- Low self-esteem
- Anger and hostility
- Confrontations with bill collectors
- Drug or alcohol abuse
- Undesirable personal relationships
- Verbal abuse toward others
- Increased physical illness
- Diminished physical activity
- Loss of friendships

    a. eight to ten
    b. five to seven
    c. two to four
    d. none or one

Entrepreneurship Test

1. Many who confront the Stay or Leave dilemma toss around the idea of going into business for themselves. For most, it never goes much beyond the "idea" stage, but there are some who will take the chance.

    Unfortunately, the odds are 3 to 1 that they will not be successful. Chances are they're fooling themselves. It's sad, but true—few have what it takes to turn a dream into a going venture. To determine whether you have the skills needed to be an entrepreneur or would be better off staying where you are, honestly answer the following.

    You've made a mistake. Do you usually . . .

    a. take the responsibility for your errors?
    b. find that someone or something else (perhaps fate) caused the error?

2. To be successful in your own business you need an overabundance of _____.

    a. luck
    b. money
    c. hard work
    d. patience

3. Generally speaking, are you . . .

    a. dissatisfied with the status quo?
    b. content with the way things are?

4. Would others who know you say you are . . .

    a. a doer?
    b. a manager?
    c. a planner?
    d. a strategist?

5. Your primary motivation for starting your own business would be . . .

    a. to make money.
    b. to more fully use your high level of energy.
    c. because working for someone else doesn't seem to work for you.
    d. to become famous.

Gabe Mirkin, M.D., is a practicing physician and nationally known expert on fitness whose articles appear frequently in popular and scientific publications. He spoke about expanding his career beyond his medical practice.

"I realized that once you've seen a hundred cases of hay fever, you've seen them all. I wanted other challenges.

"While hosting the national A.A.U. cross-country championships in D.C., I went to the *Washington Post* and asked for more publicity for the event. They laughed at me.

"I took a chance. I offered to write the article even though I felt it would take forever to do because at the time my writing wasn't worth a damn. Not only did they publish that article but gave me a regular column every Thursday.

"A similar thing happened when my friend, a professor in the Department of Physical Education at the University of Maryland, asked me to teach a course in sportsmedicine. Again, I took a chance. I taught for a couple of years and the course became one of the most popular at the school. Then I used my notes and wrote *The Sportsmedicine Book;* it became a national best seller, was translated into twelve languages and sold half a million copies. While on a book-promotional tour, CBS radio offered me a daily one-hour show.

"These experiences have shown me that if you are willing to take a chance, others may do the same. I'm glad I did."

6. Do you enjoy picking up bits and pieces of information about subjects that are not in your area of expertise?

   a. Not usually. There's little sense in cluttering my mind with data I'll most likely never use.
   b. Yes. You never know when these facts will be useful.

7. You're in your own business and are talking with a potential customer who has obviously misunderstood what you have said. At this time, it is best for you to say . . .

   a. "I guess I didn't make it clear."
   b. "Pardon me, but you're mistaken about that."
   c. "I'm not sure, but I think you misunderstood me."
   d. "That's not what I said. I think you're somewhat confused about that."

8. People who consider the entrepreneurial career path should select as a role model a person . . .

   a. who appears to be in complete control of his or her destiny.
   b. who can attain power and use it judiciously.
   c. who has a decidedly deep understanding of the nation's present economy.
   d. who values accumulation of money more than anything else.

9. Which turns you on to do your best?

   a. The excitement of new challenges, handling the unknown, making new friends.
   b. The comfort of knowing what others expect of you, a routine you can handle successfully.

10. Nearly all authors of self-help career books, assertiveness trainers and motivational speakers repeatedly emphasize the positive value of setting personal and work-related goals. An assistant vice-president of a large city bank said, "As far as career planning goes, I like to formulate a good, detailed plan of action based upon my goals. Then I stick closely to it. If the results are not what I planned for, I go back and draw up another plan of action."
    Do you . . .

    a. basically agree with her approach?
    b. basically disagree with her approach?

11. Have you recently said to yourself, "It bothers me that I've made a few mistakes lately that have cost my company money?"

    a. yes
    b. no
    c. does not apply

12. During your adult life, have you ever lived more than six months without a steady regular income?

    a. yes
    b. no

13. Although your field may not be akin to the samples in this question, the concept is what counts. Is your dissatisfaction similar to that of the salesperson who had such a great performance record the company made her sales manager—a job she does not like, or the hands-on construction engineer who has been "promoted" and now sells projects to state governments?

    a. yes
    b. no

Jerome Navies is Director of CBS Radio Stations News Service, in Washington, D.C. He began working for CBS at Los Angeles's KNX Radio in 1972 and was there for eight years before circumstances made him consider a change. As he recalls:

"It was the summer of 1980 when I started to have a long-distance relationship with a woman I eventually married. A woman who, at the time, played a big part in my decision to leave KNX Radio. She was from the Washington, D.C. area, and I was living in Los Angeles when we met. About that same time I was beginning to focus in on what I really wanted to do. I had done everything I could at KNX. The next question was, 'Could I be happy working in D.C.?' I would have to find a job there since she was not going to move to California.

"I gave it some serious thought and decided to sell myself on the move. But I was concerned about how I would be received. Ten years was a long time to be out of the job market. That was a big fear. What were people going to say about my credentials? Where was I going to work? More questions that needed answers.

"I started to map out a strategy—how to get this next job, how to make it a positive process. The feeling was like you know where the next step is but you're looking for the staircase. And I was on my way to find out how to get there.

"I turned to my boss. We had worked together for a long time. He made some calls, and gave me contacts in Washington, who were involved in news. I called, sent out letters and resumes, and began to

---

14. If you were running your own business, and a potential client you had identified as one of the "ten most-wanted" prospects consistently refused to do business with you, would you . . .

    a.   continue the assault, confident he would eventually "come around"?
    b.   shift your focus efforts elsewhere, and think "the hell with him"?
    c.   tell him outright, "I don't know what the problem is, but I want to try one more time"?

15. Do you experience a feeling of importance when you tell a new acquaintance where you work?

    a.   yes
    b.   no

16. Is the following statement true for you? "Doing my job well gives me a good feeling."

    a.   yes
    b.   no

commute every other month to D.C. Fortunately, I was able to work out of the office I am now in charge of. I had a very good relationship with the staff at our Washington Bureau. Once I arrived here, I felt confident that I was going to get something worthwhile. It was just a matter of time. In fact, the more interviews I did, the better I got.

"I talked to everyone and anybody I could find in the industry. At one point, I got a very favorable response, it was a great job offer, a chance to make my move to the East Coast, which was my number one goal. But the money wasn't right, it would mean a pay cut. And I had to wrestle with that thought for a while. You know, for ego and economic sake you never want to go backwards. It was like 'how badly do I want to make this move?'

"I know sometimes you may have to make a sacrifice to get what you really want. I didn't really want to take a pay cut, but I was getting to that point where I was beginning to think about it—and then I said flatly, 'No.' I kept up with my contacts, and then, one day, it happened just like that. The head of CBS Radio Stations News Service in Washington got a promotion and moved to a Chicago station. His position was just up my alley, it required the experience I had, I knew the person doing the hiring, the job was tailor-made for me, the offer came, and I took it.

"As things turned out, I'm glad I decided to continue working until the right opportunity came up. There's a lot of truth to 'It's easier to get a job when you have one.' You have time to let it happen. You allow yourself time for good things to happen to you."

17. Sure you work hard. Yet the job doesn't seem to exhaust you beyond a reasonable degree. You still have enough time to spend with family, friends or hobbies.

    a. true
    b. false

18. In previous positions you've held, after six months on the job, has your presence been tangibly and specifically acknowledged by someone in management *above* the level of your immediate supervisor?

    a. yes
    b. no

19. Would you say that your choice of career or job is too important a factor in your life to be limited to such considerations as pay and perks?

    a. Yes, there are other important considerations.
    b. No, pay and perks are the principal ones for me to consider.

Paul Steinle is President of United Press International. He is also a former President and Chief Executive Officer of Data Broadcasting Corporation and Financial News Network (FNN). Author of more than twenty TV and radio documentaries, and coauthor of Commune: Life in Rural China, Mr. Steinle received the Overseas Press Club citation for excellence in radio reporting in Vietnam, 1972.

"Recently, I was the president of a subsidiary of the Financial News Network. I left to come here to U.P.I., a company that hasn't made money for decades. It's been in trouble for years. I consider this a high challenge. What's more important, I'm in a different stage of my life now, the pay-back stage. I'm interested in doing something that serves the field I'm in and this does it. There are certainly more fun things to do than running a company which I'm doing today . . . like being out there and doing stories. But then again, the idea of replenishing the resources that make this company successful benefits everyone. It benefits the news industry since U.P.I. gives this country another source of information. It benefits the world when we collect information and then direct it back to the world. That's very exciting."

Interview
Caspar Willard
Weinberger
Publisher of
Forbes *and former*
Secretary of
Defense

Caspar Willard Weinberger served as Secretary of Defense from 1981 until 1987. In March 1988 President Reagan appointed him a member of the President's Foreign Intelligence Advisory Board and a member of the National Economic Commission. Before he became Secretary of Defense, Mr. Weinberger was director of several companies—PepsiCo, Inc., New York; Quaker Oats Co., Chicago; and the Bechtel Group, San Francisco. In January 1989 Mr. Weinberger became Publisher of Forbes magazine.

"I've had quite a few transitions in my lifetime. I have moved from the private to the public sector and back a number of times: from law school to Army, to law clerk, to lawyer, to legislator, back to lawyer, to Director of Finance in California, to various cabinet and regulatory posts in Washington, back to lawyer, to Secretary of Defense, and now back again to the private sector. These changes have been like transplanting trees and shrubs, which in horticulture, is supposed to be very good for them. However, these moves required a great deal of effort on the part of my family, and they can indeed be quite disruptive of personal comfort. My wife thinks I may have overdone the transplanting process, but I think it is a good thing to pull up your roots and replant them from time to time."

In downtown D.C., in the glossy Washington Square complex, is Duke Zeibert's, a restaurant favored by celebrities, politicians and the wheelers and dealers of big business. Not all of us start out as junior executives. Duke Zeibert told Linda of a time early in his career when he had to decide whether to stay and face the music.

Interview
Duke Zeibert
Restaurateur

"I have a real good story, a true story. Are you ready? God almighty! This happened in the early forties.

"There used to be a place in Florida where I worked as a head waiter, maitre d', and manager. When the war started I came to Washington, with the owners, and worked for them here.

"And in those days I would bet on anything . . . on two raindrops coming down the window. Anyway, there was a very big bookmaker that used to come every Monday for lunch at the restaurant and leave an envelope with money. At dinnertime somebody would come by and pick it up. One such Monday a good fat envelope was left with a lot of money inside and I put it in my pocket. Some people came in that day who owned horses and I decided to go with them to the racetrack.

"It didn't take much time to lose the little I had to spend. The guy I was with was so high on this horse in the next race, but I was already broke when I happened to remember the envelope sitting in my pocket. I had the nerve of a burglar, more nerve than Dick Tracy. I said, 'I'm going to take a shot.' I opened the envelope and there was two thousand, five hundred dollars. I went to the window and put it all down.

"I don't have to tell you—the horse lost, and I went back to work. I knew the guy was coming to pick up the envelope. Mind you, I was no kid . . . I was in my early thirties. And here I am waiting for 'Gut Time.' I had to make a decision. I was free, had no obligations whatsoever. I thought, 'Should I just pick up and leave or stay and face the consequences?' Then I started to reason—'Hey, this guy is a gambler, he'll understand. I'm going to tell him exactly what happened.' Sure enough, the guy came back to pick up the money, and I told him, 'Just tell Bunny to call me.' Bunny the bookmaker called. He said, 'Don't worry, kid, I'll see you tomorrow.' He turned up with another man. Bunny said, 'This man is going to loan you two thousand, five hundred dollars—he's called a shylock.' Bunny got his money right away. And me? I just paid this shylock and paid him I don't know how many hundreds of dollars more.

"I'm happy I made that decision, because right afterwards, my luck changed. I met this nice young lady, got married, and had a lovely family. And that's it! Every word is absolutely true."

20. For each of the statements below, assign points as follows:

    1 point if you strongly disagree
    4 points if you neither agree nor disagree
    7 points if you strongly agree

Points

- If you take many chances, you often make costly mistakes. _____
- Managers should be more willing to take risks. _____
- I find I often have to make risky decisions based upon limited information. _____
- Most of my accomplishments are the results of cautious decisions I've made. _____
- In my current company, too many approvals are needed for minor decisions. _____
- Sometimes the best decisions are based on hunches. _____
- I often worry what my job will be five years from now. _____

Total: _____

Your total is . . .

    a. 28 or more
    b. 27 or less

21. Do you tolerate scrutiny well?

    a. yes
    b. no

22. Do you enjoy or take pride in the automatic prestige that your title or company's name bestows?

    a. yes
    b. no

23. If your boss, known for his jovial and backslapping attitude, routinely passes you without greeting you in the halls, do you:

    a. wonder why he doesn't and ask someone you trusted what to do?
    b. attempt to avoid passing him in the hall?
    c. assume he doesn't like you?
    d. wish he'd give you a pat, but go on with your normal business?

24. In the past six months, have you attended self-improvement courses or seminars that have little to do with your work or industry?

    a. yes
    b. no

Job-changing Test

1. The "grass-is-always-greener" syndrome (thinking that any other situation will be better than what you have) can affect highly ambitious people and anyone who wants to escape from a discouraging work situation. And while it is true that it's often advisable to leave one job to go to a more responsible one, some people act impatiently and rush their career progress before they're truly ready.

   Are you ready? Here's one way to find out. Just complete the following self-rating chart. On a scale of 1 (very low) to 10 (truly outstanding), realistically rate yourself on the characteristics listed below.

   Rating

   - Demonstrated leadership ability _____
   - Ability to communicate ideas clearly _____
   - Energy level on an average day _____
   - Ability to ingest information, analyze it and make decisions _____
   - Willingness to take risks _____
   - Ability to work without close direct supervision _____
   - Knowledge of current industry conditions _____
   - Ability to exude enthusiasm and motivate others _____
   - Proven ability to be well organized _____
   - Mentally healthy _____
   - Ability to work effectively when under pressure to get things done fast _____
   - Willingness to be responsible for the work done by others _____

   Now total your self-ratings. *Total:* _____

   Select the most appropriate of the following.

   a. You are thinking about leaving to get a job one or two rungs up the ladder and your self-rating total lies between 60 and 90.
   b. You are thinking about leaving to get a job one or two rungs up the ladder and your self-rating total is above 90.
   c. You are thinking about leaving and expect to get a comparable job in another company. Your self-rating total lies between 40 and 80.
   d. Your self-rating total is below 60.
   e. Your self-rating total is above 96.

Questions 2 and 3 pertain to the following scenario.

You've known Debra for nearly eight years. And during that time have become very good friends.

Two years ago when you moved into another department, your friendship continued. You still managed to have lunch together once a week, plus you meet every Wednesday night at the local drama-club meeting. You'd say you probably know Debra better than anyone else.

Lately, however, you sense Debra has something on her mind. She seems somewhat troubled. And she tells you about a problem she is having at work.

As things turn out, Debra's problem is very similar to the one you're experiencing at work.

2. Could you give her advice that might help her solve the problem?

    a. yes
    b. no

3. Would your solution to her problem mean that she _____ her present position?

    a. stays on
    b. leaves

4. Do you agree or disagree with the following statement? Success breeds success; ambition breeds distrust.

    a. agree
    b. disagree

5. Furthermore, do you agree or disagree: Not to succeed means to fail.

    a. agree
    b. disagree

6. How difficult would it be for you to find a similar job in your industry?

    a. very difficult
    b. not any more difficult than it is in most industries
    c. relatively easy

7. One friend of ours is truly a workaholic, a compulsive young lady who dots all her "*i*'s" and crosses all her "*t*'s." And when she's done, without taking a breath, she goes gunning for her next set of tasks.

J. Carter Brown has been Director of the National Gallery of Art in Washington, D.C., for over twenty years.

"I think that the basic thought is if you can stay at a job long enough you can have your efforts become cumulative. What you can do over a long period of time is to build—whatever it is—brick by brick. I find that a lot of energy goes into starting a job and digging the big hole and planning the foundation, and then more often than not, people leave before the building, as it were, is completed. Personally, it's terribly exciting to have been around long enough to have had some long-range visions and goals and find them to be reachable and actually happen. . . . One feels that one's energies have all been laid end-to-end so as to try to add up to the longest possible line."

Another friend is a steady, hardworking guy who does his job well from nine to five, but resents being forced to work late.

What about you? Are you . . .

    a. a nine-to-fiver who is in a job that often requires you to work overtime?

    b. a workaholic who is shunned by fellow employees because the five-day week or the five o'clock bell means nothing?

    c. someone whose current time needs are met by the structure of your job?

8. We've all heard "T.G.I.F." But, believe it or not, there's also "T.G.I.M." for those really excited about what they do. Let's determine where you stand.

    Select the one of the following that *best* typifies your feelings upon awakening on an average workday.

    a. "Things are really humming at work. Can't wait to get into today's project."

    b. "Most of the time, but not always, it's off to work I go!"

    c. "Sure, I gotta go, but I'd rather do almost anything else."

    d. "Wish I could call in sick again. I hate getting up and going to work."

9. Simply put, more and more you dread going to work more than you look forward to it.

    a. true

    b. false

10. Complete the following sentence by selecting the one alternative that *best* pertains to you. "I guess I'm like most people. I'd like to get a better job, *but* _____."

    a. I'd be giving up my seniority and the benefits I've accumulated over the years

    b. I know what I've got now; maybe I'd just be going from the frying pan into the fire

    c. I'd have to be thoroughly convinced the new position is genuinely better

    d. I'd be losing all the friends I've made here throughout the years

11. In today's business world, it's quite fashionable for company spokespersons to declare the company's honest concern for its employees. Human resource departments are enlarged, special day-care centers are created and fitness centers are provided. Attentiveness to employees is all well and good, but the business of business is still to make a profit; the prime purpose of a service-related organization is to serve its constituents. In this context, your superiors still evaluate your productivity. And your level of productivity is directly related to the stay or leave puzzle.

Are you putting in less effort yet producing as much as (or more than) others with similar responsibilities; are you working longer and producing less; or are you staying just about even with others?

    a. I put in less effort but produce more.

    b. I work longer/harder and produce the same as others.

12. Okay, let's say you work fairly hard. You put consistent effort into your job. You faithfully try to carry out your responsibilities. Despite these positive attributes, your career has run into a brick wall. You seem to be going nowhere.

You are not alone. When many of your peers experience this frustration, they soon contemplate quitting their job and starting anew. They hope a brand new start will bring success and change their luck.

But luck is not usually the missing ingredient. We have found, more often than not, that a repeated lack of success occurs because people tend to overlook their own shortcomings.

It's not easy to see yourself as others see you, especially in those areas in which you are not strong. It's even harder to admit these stifling weaknesses.

Here's your chance to see how many possibly self-hindering problems you'll acknowledge.

Place a check mark in the appropriate column.

- I blame my boss for my current career problems. ___ ___
- I blame the state of the national economy for my current career problems. ___ ___
- I have a lot of trouble accepting criticism, even constructive criticism. ___ ___
- My short-term goals are way beyond my current reach. ___ ___
- Usually, I brood over a past mistake. ___ ___
- I never seem to have the time to do the things I want to do. ___ ___
- I rarely look for new experiences in my life. ___ ___
- I'm happy and comfortable with what is familiar. ___ ___
- It's hard for me to ask others for help because they might think I'm incompetent. ___ ___
- Truthfully, I've just floated through my career without much planning. ___ ___
- My philosophy is . . . "Shortcomings? The easiest way to deal with them is to forget them." ___ ___
- My work is the only thing of real importance in my life. ___ ___
- When I get into a competitive situation, I usually back down. ___ ___
- I've lived in the real world and have learned that you must always be on guard. You really cannot trust most people. ___ ___
- I've read all these career books, gone to training classes and lectures. And I've come to the conclusion that I probably won't change. ___ ___

Step One: total the number of check marks in the "That's Me" column. _____

Step Two: total the number of check marks in the "Not Me" column. _____

Step Three: subtract Step Two total from Step One total. (If the result is less than zero, use zero.) _____

Use the numerical value you obtain in Step Three and mark your answer sheet accordingly.

   a. zero
   b. two
   c. four
   d. six or more

Doug Fraser was President of the United Auto Workers from 1977 to 1983. During a recent visit by Barry and Linda to Mr. Fraser's office at Columbia University Business School, where he is Labor Leader in Residence, he told of his opportunity to run for the U.S. Senate and represent the State of Michigan. He asked himself, "Should I stay in my current position or leave to begin the campaign trail?" Fraser decided to stay. When asked what factors influenced his thinking, he replied:

"I had to decide how I could play the most meaningful role and have the greatest impact on American society. If I were fortunate enough to have been elected I would have started as a junior senator and it would have taken several years to get seniority and a position of considerable influence. You could say . . . senators certainly are influential, but there are a hundred of them. There's only one President of the U.A.W."

13. Is there any reason pertaining to your family (a physically ill parent, the importance of your spouse's work, etc.) that would prevent you from relocating, if necessary?

    a. yes
    b. no

14. React to the following statements. Most of the jobs having more responsibility and rewards that people get didn't exist in the first place. Highly qualified people can often create jobs where none seem to be openly offered.

    a. You must be kidding. I don't believe that.
    b. Sounds reasonable. I believe it.

15. Would you risk a month's salary and time to land a job worthy of your talents?

    a. yes
    b. no

16. You learn that a new and exciting position has been created where you work. Which would you do?

    a. Actively lobby for the job and emphasize your qualifications.
    b. Apply for the job and threaten that you'll leave if you don't get it.
    c. Work longer and harder with hopes of being selected.

17. Sure it's true that everyone has an occasional "bad day" at work. But (be honest!) how often do you feel irritable when you get home?

a. very often
b. occasionally
c. quite infrequently

18. Let's say you've been invited to a social event and you learn that many of the guests who are "big shots" in your industry will be there. You don't want to go alone, but for a variety of reasons beyond your control it looks like you have no other choice. What now?

    a. You go anyway.
    b. You go but stay close to those you know.
    c. You stay home.

19. Whether you're in management, advertising, research, production or whatever, the big question is: "Do you whistle while you work?"

    a. yes
    b. no

20. Complete the following by selecting the one alternative that *best* pertains to you. "My background and experience suggest I'm probably ready for a new, more rewarding job. But job-hunting can be a real pain in the neck. The one part of the process that inhibits me most is . . .

    a. deciding what I want to do next."
    b. handling the interview correctly."
    c. the effort of overcoming my self-imposed inertia and getting started."
    d. finding job leads."
    e. nothing. I'm ready to get started!"

21. Which of the following comes closest to describing how you got your present position?

    a. "I urgently needed a job, you know, for the money. This position was offered to me, so I grabbed it."
    b. "I throughly investigated many career opportunities and chose this one with my eyes wide open. But now, I'm bored with it all."
    c. "A friend of mine worked here. She knew there was another job vacancy, so I applied. And here I am."
    d. "During my college years, I truly wanted a job like this someday. But now that I've got it, I realize it's not exactly what I want."

22. Was your last job change a _____ ?

    a. promotion
    b. lateral change
    c. demotion

Mary Futrell is President of the National Education Association (NEA). As she tells it, the move from teacher to full-time officer in a national organization involved some serious considerations.

"In 1979 I was serving on the NEA board of directors as the At-large Minority Director. Many people approached me to run for NEA Secretary Treasurer. That meant I would have to take a leave of absence from my teaching job to become a full-time officer. In making my decision, I had to think about a number of things.

"The first one, my family. I'm married. How would this position affect my family? Secondly, would my school district be willing to give me a leave of absence and for how long? Would they be willing to guarantee me a position once I completed my term of office? A third thought went through my mind—'Could I get elected?' When you're going for a position like that—let's face it, you have feelings, you have an ego. 'What if I run for this office and I lose? What happens if I win?'

"So, after a lot of self-debate, I sat down and talked to my husband about it. He said I should run, but not to get involved unless I was willing to give the position my full commitment. I had to think about all the time I would have to spend away from home, if elected.

"I had to look at Mary, the person, because believe it or not, I was really very shy. I'm not very good at meeting people or being outgoing. I knew that if I was going to get involved, I would have to find the courage to meet people and shake hands, ask for support, explain who I was and why I was running. However, after I got over the initial discomfort, it worked out okay. I learned to give speeches, to say what I wanted to say in a matter of just two or three minutes; how to answer questions off the top of my head. I learned how to deal with people who didn't like me and weren't supportive. I had to convince the people I would be a better candidate, which is like selling yourself as a product. And you have to be able to package this product to persuade people to support you. The fact that I was a woman was used against me. The fact that I was a southerner was used against me. In addition to trying to address the issues, I had to deal with all these 'personality' kinds of issues.

"My school district was very supportive and granted my request for leave. I was fortunate I didn't have to move. I didn't have disruptions in my private life, like leaving my family home in another state. Most importantly, my husband was very supportive, and that indeed made it all work out fine."

Knight Kiplinger is Publisher and Editor-in-Chief of Changing Times *magazine. He is also Vice-President for Publications of Kiplinger Washington Editors, Inc. What Linda recalls most vividly about Mr. Kiplinger's office is the solid, mahogany-toned stuffed leather couch. It felt so comfortable that she was uncomfortable feeling so relaxed on the job. In the interview, he spoke of the value of getting experience outside the family business.*

Interview
Knight Kiplinger
Changing Times
and Kiplinger
Washington
Editors, Inc.

"When I look at a resume, and I see somebody who has moved every two years, I have to confess it occurs to me that person hasn't paid back his employer for the effort and expense of training. The pattern suggests someone who probably takes more from the company (experience, instruction and guidance) than he gives back.

"It's not that anybody owes the employer any particular length of service, or any commitment to stay five or seven years. If someone has worked hard each day and has rendered valuable service, nobody begrudges that person the desire to move on.

"I had three jobs in thirteen years, before finally joining the family business. I viewed each of these jobs and each job change as a building block—a foundation of experience for eventually joining the family business.

"I don't think any young person should join a family business as his first job. A young person will never find out the true measure of his talents—what he is worth—in an objective and unbiased way if he goes to work for the family business at the age of twenty-one, right from college. 'I want you to treat Junior the same way you treat any employee,' the owner of the company might say to his son's or daughter's supervisor. But it doesn't matter how often he says that or how sincere he seems. The manager who is in charge of that young family member is not going to treat that person the same as every other employee. It's human nature that the middle-management person is not going to risk disapproval of the boss by suggesting the young person be fired, or that he or she doesn't have the talent for this particular work or the temperament, the particular skills the job requires. Turning it around a bit, the business does not benefit particularly from bringing in a young, inexperienced employee who will be insulated and protected by the parent.

"My father, as a young man, worked briefly with his father for a few years after World War II. They worked in this organization together. They cofounded *Changing Times* magazine. And they had some tensions. My father, on his own, decided to leave the family business, a very hard thing to do. He had the courage and the intelligence to do that. He then made it on his own, in television journalism. He developed a confidence in his own ability which would have been difficult to develop within the family business. When he returned to the Kiplinger organization eight years later, he was a stronger person and the company benefited greatly from his experience elsewhere."

Rose Narva (better known as ''The Ultimate Innkeeper'' and ''Hostess to the Rich and Famous''), is Director of the Jefferson Hotel in Washington, D.C. (former home base for the Reagan Cabinet and known as ''White House North''). She told Linda about two wonderful opportunities she received in 1985:

''I had an offer I couldn't refuse. A West Coast real-estate developer offered me my dream . . . to work with an architect, form a hotel division and be its president.

''The decision to terminate my position at the Jefferson Hotel was a difficult one. I thought about the labor of love I had put into that wonderful hotel property. I had built a devoted and committed staff that proudly worked together as a team. Leaving also led to a long-distance commute because my husband's career continued in Washington, D.C.

''But I had to take this 'once-in-a-lifetime' opportunity. However, after arriving on the West Coast, it didn't take me long to realize that being involved with real estate was not my world. I missed the hands-on experiences and day-to-day challenges hotel operations offered. So, when I had the unusual offer by my previous employer, Mr. Edward Bennett Williams, the owner of The Jefferson, to return to my former job, I had to seriously consider the option. Here I was a second time around, thinking 'Can you go back? Do I, or don't I?' And I did. I'm very happy I did.''

23. "I do my job faithfully and I'm patiently waiting for something good, like a promotion, to happen." (How often we've heard this sentiment.) Are you . . .

   a. biding your time, waiting for Aladdin's lamp to appear and the genie to grant you a promotion?
   b. actively taking the initiative to tell the people with the power what you want to do next?

24. Sometime in the past, you thought it over and decided to leave your present position. You took the necessary steps (preparing resumes and cover letters, doing interviews, engaging the services of a recruiter, visiting a career-management consultant) and landed a better job. Then, when you went to quit, your boss said he needed you. No one else could possibly do your job—you couldn't leave him now. There was some kind of emergency

Currently President and Chief Operating Officer of Loews Corporation (total revenue about $8 billion) and Chairman Emeritus of the New York Convention and Visitors Bureau, Preston Robert Tisch is also a Trustee of New York University and a Director of City Meals-on-Wheels, an organization he helped found. Here's the story behind his decision to take a leave of absence from the Loews Corporation to become Postmaster General:

"When I came here I decided I was going to stay about twenty-four months. At the end of twenty, I began to feel I had accomplished what I set out to do. That's why it was the opportune time for me to leave at that point and bring in a very good man, Tony Frank, an outstanding businessperson who could carry forward the next phase in the life of the postal operations.

"The Postal Service was in distress when I arrived. They were in trouble with Congress, major mailers, the union, and the executive branch of government. I was able to quickly change that and give these people a lot of respect back in themselves. For the first time in eighteen years, they had negotiated contracts. I was also responsible for implementing a marketing program. We had competition out there with UPS. We put a marketing sense into the company. And then I came to the conclusion that a major program was stalled because a former governor in May of 1986 was convicted of putting his hand in a till, and I got that turned around.

"I thought working for the Postal Service was a great experience . . . but like many things in life, you come, you do it, and you move on."

---

situation coming up. You began to feel guilty. So you stayed put and turned down the new job offer.

Has this ever happened to you?

a. yes
b. no

25. Congratulations! After three years at a great job, you've been promoted to a higher-level position in another department of the same company. Today is your last day at the current job. Which of the following are you most likely to do?

    a. leave early to avoid the many emotional "good-byes."
    b. make definite plans for a weekly lunch with former coworkers.
    c. prepare a brief farewell speech thanking your boss and coworkers for their friendship, support, etc.

Eddie R. White has been everything from a bombardier-navigator in World War II to Vice-President of Yamaha in Japan. From the wall-to-wall autographed pictures that decorate his home and office, one suspects he has become well acquainted with all of the rich and famous. Today he is a songwriter, producer, writer and actor. He has appeared in such movies as The Killer Elite, Manhattan *and* Annie Hall, *produced concerts and plays and written a book entitled* Yesterday's Cake.

"My experience in the military convinced me that I could do anything. I just swallowed my fears and looked straight ahead and kept going. I never give up. I'm determined and I get there.

"I wanted to write songs and get into the theatrical business, to be a producer on Broadway. I opened my office right next to Frank Sinatra's. I didn't have too much money so I had to wash the windows and floors myself . . . but I did it. I wrote songs for Frank Sinatra and all of the greats of that era. And now I have a new career. I'm an actor.

"I'm going to be a great character actor. Now, I'm the product that I'm going to sell for the first time in my life. I'm on the throne for a change. For the first time the camera is pointed at me. And I love it."

26. When you first came on board at your current job, did you take the time and exert the effort to find out about your supervisor's background (former schooling, family, personal likes or dislikes, etc.)?

    a. Yes.
    b. No, I didn't want to appear nosy.
    c. No, but I will on my next job.

27. Have you been actively seeking contacts inside or outside your company who could help you find your next job?

    a. yes
    b. no

PART 3
SCORING

Scoring Your Tests

It's time to score your tests. Before you begin, we would like to offer this suggestion: *Score them carefully.* Compute your scores with the same attention and concern you used to take each test. We assume you took the tests carefully and now do not want to spoil your efforts by scoring your answers inaccurately.

Scoring instructions for all six of the tests are exactly the same.

1. Compare your answers for each test with the corresponding scoring keys on the following pages. Each answer is assigned a value ranging from 5S to 1S (*S*tay), zero, or 1L to 5L (*L*eave).
2. Record each value on the corresponding Tally Sheet.
3. Total your Stay Points.
4. Total your Leave Points.
5. Subtract the smaller score from the larger. You now have your Net Score for that particular test.

Sample Scoring
Values/Skills Test: Stay Points 26   Leave Points 56

$$
\begin{array}{r}
56\text{L} \\
-\,26\text{S} \\
\hline
30\text{L}
\end{array}
$$
      Your Net Score = L

6. Transfer your Net Scores, as either "S" or "L," to Your Personal Profile on page 135. In this example:

Values/Skills Test ___L___

Relationships/Office Politics
Scoring Key

1. a = 3L b = 1S

2. a = 2S b = 1L

3. a = 2S b = 1L

4. a = 5L b = 3L c = 2L d = 2S

5. a = 3S b = 1S c = 1L d = 3L

6. a = 3S b = 1L

7. a = 2L b = 2S c = 2S d = 1L

8. a = 2L b = 1S c = 2S d = 1S

9. a = 1L b = 1S

10. a = 3S b = 3L c = 2S

11. a = 1L b = 1S

12. a = 3L b = 2S

13. a = 1S b = 2S c = 3L

14. a = 4L b = 4S

15. a = 1S b = 1L

16. a = 2L b = 2S c = 0

17. a = 3L b = 2S c = 0

18. a = 5S b = 3S c = 1L d = 2L

19. a = 2L b = 1S

20. a = 4S b = 2S c = 1L d = 3L

21. a = 2S b = 1S c = 2L

22. a = 2S b = 1S c = 2L

23. a = 2S b = 1S c = 2L

24. a = 2S b = 1S c = 2L

25. a = 3S b = 1S c = 2L

26. a = 1S b = 1L

27. a = 1S b = 1L

28. a = 1S b = 1L

Relationships/Office Politics
Tally Sheet

	Stay Points	*Leave Points*
1.	_____	_____
2.	_____	_____
3.	_____	_____
4.	_____	_____
5.	_____	_____
6.	_____	_____
7.	_____	_____
8.	_____	_____
9.	_____	_____
10.	_____	_____
11.	_____	_____
12.	_____	_____
13.	_____	_____
14.	_____	_____
15.	_____	_____
16.	_____	_____
17.	_____	_____
18.	_____	_____
19.	_____	_____
20.	_____	_____
21.	_____	_____
22.	_____	_____
23.	_____	_____
24.	_____	_____
25.	_____	_____
26.	_____	_____
27.	_____	_____
28.	_____	_____

29. a = 1S b = 1L

30. a = 2S b = 2L

31. a = 2S b = 2L

32. a = 3L b = 1S c = 1S

33. a = 4S b = 4L

34. a = 1S b = 1L

35. a = 2L b = 1S

36. a = 0 b = 1S

37. a = 1L b = 1S

38. a = 3L b = 2L c = 2S d = 0

39. a = 2L b = 2S c = 1S d = 0

40. a = 3L b = 2L c = 2S d = 0

41. a = 3L b = 2L c = 1S d = 3S

42. a = 2S b = 3S c = 1L d = 0

43. a = 2S b = 4L c = 1S d = 0

44. a = 3S b = 1L c = 2S

45. a = 5L b = 2L c = 4S d = 5S

46. a = 3S b = 3L c = 5S d = 0

47. a = 5L b = 1S

48. a = 2L b = 1S

49. a = 1S b = 0

50. a = 3L b = 3S

51. a = 4L b = 2L c = 2S d = 0

52. a = 2S b = 2L

53. a = 3S b = 1S c = 2S d = 2L

54. a = 2S b = 2S c = 2L d = 3L

Relationships/Office Politics
Tally Sheet (cont.)

	Stay Points	Leave Points
29.	_____	_____
30.	_____	_____
31.	_____	_____
32.	_____	_____
33.	_____	_____
34.	_____	_____
35.	_____	_____
36.	_____	_____
37.	_____	_____
38.	_____	_____
39.	_____	_____
40.	_____	_____
41.	_____	_____
42.	_____	_____
43.	_____	_____
44.	_____	_____
45.	_____	_____
46.	_____	_____
47.	_____	_____
48.	_____	_____
49.	_____	_____
50.	_____	_____
51.	_____	_____
52.	_____	_____
53.	_____	_____
54.	_____	_____

Totals

Stay	Leave	Net Score
_____	_____	_____

Values/Skills
Scoring Key

1. a = 5S b = 3S c = 1S d = 2L e = 4L
2. a = 1L b = 1S
3. a = 2L b = 3S
4. a = 1L b = 2S
5. a = 2L b = 2S
6. a = 1L b = 1S
7. a = 3S b = 3L c = 1L
8. a = 1S b = 2S c = 4L
9. a = 2L b = 1S c = 4S
10. a = 5S b = 1S c = 4L
11. a = 2S b = 1L
12. a = 1S b = 1L
13. a = 3S b = 1L
14. a = 1S b = 1L
15. a = 4S b = 5L
16. a = 1S b = 1L
17. a = 3S b = 2L
18. a = 1S b = 1S c = 1S d = 1S e = 3L f = 5L
19. a = 4S b = 3S c = 3L d = 5L
20. a = 3S b = 2L
21. a = 4S b = 3S c = 1S d = 2L e = 5L
22. a = 3L b = 1S
23. a = 2S b = 2L
24. a = 1L b = 1S

Values/Skills
Tally Sheet

	Stay Points	Leave Points
1.		
2.		
3.		
4.		
5.		
6.		
7.		
8.		
9.		
10.		
11.		
12.		
13.		
14.		
15.		
16.		
17.		
18.		
19.		
20.		
21.		
22.		
23.		
24.		

25. a = 3L   b = 1S

26. a = 3S   b = 1L   c = 3L   d = 4S

27. a = 5S   b = 1S   c = 2L

28. a = 4S   b = 1S   c = 2L

29. a = 2L   b = 2S   c = 3L

30. a = 2L   b = 3S

31. a = 1L   b = 2S

32. a = 1L   b = 1S

33. a = 1S   b = 1L   c = 1S

34. a = 4S   b = 2L   c = 2L   d = 1S   e = 3L

35. a = 3S   b = 2S   c = 1S   d = 3L

36. a = 2S   b = 2L

37. a = 4S   b = 3L   c = 1S

38. a = 4S   b = 3L

39. a = 3L   b = 3S

40. a = 3S   b = 3L

41. a = 3S   b = 3L

42. a = 3S   b = 1S   c = 3L

43. a = 3S   b = 2S   c = 1S   d = 3L

44. a = 2S   b = 1S   c = 1L   d = 2L

45. a = 1L   b = 1S

46. a = 2L   b = 1S

47. a = 1L   b = 1S

48. a = 2S   b = 2L

Values/Skills
Tally Sheet (cont.)

	Stay Points	Leave Points
25.	_____	_____
26.	_____	_____
27.	_____	_____
28.	_____	_____
29.	_____	_____
30.	_____	_____
31.	_____	_____
32.	_____	_____
33.	_____	_____
34.	_____	_____
35.	_____	_____
36.	_____	_____
37.	_____	_____
38.	_____	_____
39.	_____	_____
40.	_____	_____
41.	_____	_____
42.	_____	_____
43.	_____	_____
44.	_____	_____
45.	_____	_____
46.	_____	_____
47.	_____	_____
48.	_____	_____

Totals

Stay	Leave	Net Score
_____	_____	_____

Company/Rewards
Scoring Key

1. a = 1S   b = 2L

2. a = 3S   b = 1S   c = 2L

3. a = 3S   b = 1L

4. a = 1S   b = 1L

5. a = 4S   b = 2S   c = 4L

6. a = 2S   b = 1S   c = 3L

7. a = 1S   b = 1L

8. a = 3S   b = 2L

9. a = 3S   b = 3L

10. a = 3S   b = 3L

11. a = 2L   b = 2S

12. a = 2S   b = 2L

13. a = 3L   b = 2S

14. a = 0   b = 4S   c = 3S   d = 4L

15. a = 4L   b = 2S   c = 1L

16. a = 3S   b = 1L   c = 3L

17. a = 1S   b = 2L

18. a = 1S   b = 2L

19. a = 2S   b = 3L

20. a = 3S   b = 2L

21. a = 2S   b = 2L   c = 1S

Company/Rewards
Tally Sheet

	Stay Points	Leave Points
1.	_____	_____
2.	_____	_____
3.	_____	_____
4.	_____	_____
5.	_____	_____
6.	_____	_____
7.	_____	_____
8.	_____	_____
9.	_____	_____
10.	_____	_____
11.	_____	_____
12.	_____	_____
13.	_____	_____
14.	_____	_____
15.	_____	_____
16.	_____	_____
17.	_____	_____
18.	_____	_____
19.	_____	_____
20.	_____	_____
21.	_____	_____

22. a = 0   b = 2S   c = 2L

23. a = 2S   b = 2L

24. a = 1S   b = 2L

25. a = 5L   b = 4L   c = 2L   d = 2S   e = 5S

26. a = 1L   b = 1S

27. a = 4L   b = 2S

28. a = 3L   b = 3S

29. a = 3L   b = 1S

30. a = 2L   b = 1L   c = 1S   d = 2S

31. a = 2S   b = 1S   c = 1L   d = 2L

32. a = 2S   b = 1S   c = 1L   d = 2L

33. a = 2L   b = 1L   c = 1S   d = 2S

34. a = 2L   b = 1L   c = 1S   d = 2S

35. a = 2S   b = 1S   c = 1L   d = 2L

36. a = 1S   b = 1S   c = 1S   d = 1L

37. a = 1L   b = 1S

38. a = 2S   b = 2L

39. a = 2L   b = 2S

40. a = 1L   b = 2S

41. a = 5S   b = 5L

42. a = 2S   b = 3L   c = 2S

Company/Rewards
Tally Sheet (cont.)

	Stay Points	Leave Points
22.	_____	_____
23.	_____	_____
24.	_____	_____
25.	_____	_____
26.	_____	_____
27.	_____	_____
28.	_____	_____
29.	_____	_____
30.	_____	_____
31.	_____	_____
32.	_____	_____
33.	_____	_____
34.	_____	_____
35.	_____	_____
36.	_____	_____
37.	_____	_____
38.	_____	_____
39.	_____	_____
40.	_____	_____
41.	_____	_____
42.	_____	_____

Totals

Stay	Leave	Net Score
_____	_____	_____

Stress
Scoring Key

1. a = 3S   b = 1L   c = 2L

2. a = 5L   b = 3L   c = 2L   d = 3S

3. a = 5L   b = 3L   c = 1L   d = 3S

4. a = 5L   b = 2L   c = 2S   d = 5S

5. a = 1S   b = 1L

6. a = 4L   b = 2L   c = 2S   d = 4S

7. a = 1L   b = 1S

8. a = 1L   b = 1S

9. a = 3L   b = 3S

10. a = 3L   b = 2S

11. a = 5S   b = 3S   c = 1S   d = 4L

12. a = 3L   b = 1L   c = 1S   d = 3S

13. a = 3S   b = 1S   c = 1L   d = 3L

14. a = 3S   b = 1S   c = 1L   d = 3L

15. a = 2L   b = 2S

16. a = 5S   b = 4S   c = 1S   d = 5L

17. a = 4L   b = 3L   c = 1L   d = 3S

Stress
Tally Sheet

	Stay Points	Leave Points
1.	_____	_____
2.	_____	_____
3.	_____	_____
4.	_____	_____
5.	_____	_____
6.	_____	_____
7.	_____	_____
8.	_____	_____
9.	_____	_____
10.	_____	_____
11.	_____	_____
12.	_____	_____
13.	_____	_____
14.	_____	_____
15.	_____	_____
16.	_____	_____
17.	_____	_____

Totals

Stay	Leave	Net Score
_____	_____	_____

Entrepreneurship
Scoring Key

1. a = 2L   b = 2S
2. a = 1S   b = 1S   c = 1L   d = 1S
3. a = 3L   b = 2S
4. a = 2L   b = 1S   c = 1S   d = 1S
5. a = 2S   b = 1S   c = 2L   d = 2S
6. a = 2S   b = 2L
7. a = 2L   b = 1S   c = 1S   d = 2S
8. a = 2L   b = 1S   c = 1S   d = 1S
9. a = 2L   b = 2S
10. a = 2L   b = 2S
11. a = 2S   b = 2L   c = 0
12. a = 3L   b = 3S
13. a = 1L   b = 1S
14. a = 3S   b = 2L   c = 1S
15. a = 3S   b = 2L
16. a = 2S   b = 2L
17. a = 2S   b = 2L
18. a = 3L   b = 3S
19. a = 2L   b = 4S
20. a = 3L   b = 3S
21. a = 3L   b = 3S
22. a = 4S   b = 3L
23. a = 2S   b = 2S   c = 2S   d = 2L
24. a = 3L   b = 3S

Entrepreneurship
Tally Sheet

	Stay Points	Leave Points
1.	_____	_____
2.	_____	_____
3.	_____	_____
4.	_____	_____
5.	_____	_____
6.	_____	_____
7.	_____	_____
8.	_____	_____
9.	_____	_____
10.	_____	_____
11.	_____	_____
12.	_____	_____
13.	_____	_____
14.	_____	_____
15.	_____	_____
16.	_____	_____
17.	_____	_____
18.	_____	_____
19.	_____	_____
20.	_____	_____
21.	_____	_____
22.	_____	_____
23.	_____	_____
24.	_____	_____

Totals

Stay	Leave	Net Score
_____	_____	_____

Job-changing
Scoring Key

1. a = 2L   b = 4L   c = 2L   d = 3S   e = 4L

2. a = 2S   b = 1L

3. a = 4S   b = 4L

4. a = 2S   b = 2L

5. a = 2S   b = 2L

6. a = 3S   b = 0   c = 2L

7. a = 2L   b = 2L   c = 3S

8. a = 4S   b = 2S   c = 2L   d = 4L

9. a = 3L   b = 2S

10. a = 4S   b = 3S   c = 2L   d = 2S

11. a = 3L   b = 3S

12. a = 4L   b = 2L   c = 2S   d = 4S

13. a = 3S   b = 3L

14. a = 2S   b = 2L

15. a = 3L   b = 3S

16. a = 3L   b = 1L   c = 2S

17. a = 4L   b = 2L   c = 2S

18. a = 2L   b = 1L   c = 3S

19. a = 1S   b = 1L

20. a = 3S   b = 1S   c = 4S   d = 1L   e = 4L

21. a = 2L   b = 2S   c = 1L   d = 1S

22. a = 3L   b = 1L   c = 1S

23. a = 5S   b = 3L

24. a = 2S   b = 2L

25. a = 1S   b = 1S   c = 2L

26. a = 2L   b = 2S   c = 2L

27. a = 4L   b = 4S

Job-changing Tally Sheet

	Stay Points	*Leave Points*
1.	_____	_____
2.	_____	_____
3.	_____	_____
4.	_____	_____
5.	_____	_____
6.	_____	_____
7.	_____	_____
8.	_____	_____
9.	_____	_____
10.	_____	_____
11.	_____	_____
12.	_____	_____
13.	_____	_____
14.	_____	_____
15.	_____	_____
16.	_____	_____
17.	_____	_____
18.	_____	_____
19.	_____	_____
20.	_____	_____
21.	_____	_____
22.	_____	_____
23.	_____	_____
24.	_____	_____
25.	_____	_____
26.	_____	_____
27.	_____	_____

Totals

Stay	*Leave*	*Net Score*
_____	_____	_____

PART 4

WHAT YOUR SCORES REVEAL

Your Personal Profile

Place each of your Net Scores here, and designate each one either "S" or "L".

Relationships/ Office Politics	*Values/ Skills*	*Company/ Rewards*	*Stress*	*Entrepre- neurship*	*Job Changing*
_____	_____	_____	_____	_____	_____

Good. Moving on . . . Now match your profile with one listed below. First see if your profile matches one between #1 and #23. If so, read the corresponding prescription on the following pages. If not, your profile will match one in groups #24 through #27; read that corresponding prescription.

Possible Personal Profiles

Profile	Relationships/ Office Politics	Values/ Skills	Company/ Rewards	Stress	Entrepre- neurship	Job Changing
#1	S	S	S	S	S	S
#2	L	S	S	S	S	S
#3	S	L	S	S	S	S
#4	S	S	L	S	S	S
#5	S	S	S	L	S	S
#6	S	S	S	S	L	S
#7	S	S	S	S	S	L
#8	L	L	S	S	S	S
#9	L	S	L	S	S	S
#10	L	S	S	L	S	S
#11	L	S	S	S	L	S
#12	L	S	S	S	S	L
#13	S	L	L	S	S	S
#14	S	L	S	L	S	S
#15	S	L	S	S	L	S
#16	S	L	S	S	S	L
#17	S	S	L	L	S	S
#18	S	S	L	S	L	S
#19	S	S	L	S	S	L
#20	S	S	S	L	L	S
#21	S	S	S	L	S	L
#22	S	S	S	S	L	L
#23	L	L	L	S	S	S
#24	Excluding #23 above . . . any three tests, S; the remaining three, L					
#25	Any two tests, S; the remaining four, L					
#26	Any one test, S; the remaining five, L					
#27	L	L	L	L	L	L

Prescriptions

#1
Your prescription is obvious . . . stay! You've got it pretty good after all.

#2 . . . #3 . . . #4 . . . #8 . . . #9 . . . #12 . . . #13 . . . #16 . . . #19
Yes, you have manifested one or two areas of concern. And that can be exasperating, fatiguing and undesirable. However, you should now figure out if you have the power and desire to remedy the situation(s). We suggest you reexamine the questions and responses that led to your Leave Points and determine if there are actions you can take to rectify the situation(s). We also suggest that you examine the S (Stay) responses. They can often stimulate your thinking and give you some direction. If you can then set things straight at work, stay; if not, you will be packing your traveling bag soon.

#5
Stay, but keep your eyes on things. Certainly something is causing you stress, but your other scores suggest that the source of your discomfort is not job related. Suggestions: examine your health habits (diet, exercise, etc.), have a complete physical checkup and evaluate the quality of your interpersonal relationships.

#6
You've got it pretty good after all, so stay. Although you have a good intellectual grasp of what it takes to be an entrepreneur, your remaining scores do not indicate that you would significantly benefit from that move now.

#7
You've got it pretty good after all, so stay. Although you have a good intellectual grasp of the techniques of job changing, your remaining test scores do not indicate that you would significantly benefit from that move now. Simply put: It seems you have the know-how to leave, but little reason to do so.

#10 . . . #14 . . . #17 . . . #21
You have uncovered one area of concern that seems to be progressively causing you undue stress. That can be exasperating, fatiguing and certainly undesirable. Now is the time to figure out if you have the willpower and desire to first remedy the situation(s) and then monitor the effects these changes have upon your level of stress by retaking the Stress Test in two months. We suggest you reexamine the questions and your responses that led to your Leave Points and determine if there are actions you can take to rectify the situation(s). We also suggest that you examine the S (Stay) responses. They can often stimulate your thinking and give you some direction. If you can then set things straight at work, stay; if not, you'll be packing your traveling bag soon.

#11 ... #15 ... #18 ... #20 ... #22

You have uncovered one area of concern along with an understanding of entrepreneurship. You could be among those who eventually leave corporate/organizational jobs and establish a business of their own. We find that many people with one of these five profiles are not consciously aware that they possess an entrepreneurial yen. They are aware of their current dissatisfactions, but unaware that they grow out of a suppressed desire to be their own boss.

If you are willing to make the necessary sacrifices, have confidence in yourself, along with a high energy level, and have demonstrated the ability to lead others, then you might seriously consider a business of your own. If you don't have *all* these qualities, then you should seek a position within a company that is more entrepreneurial than your current one. In either case, it's time to leave.

#23

Obviously, you're in the wrong spot. You've indicated three cornerstones upon which the decision to leave is built. However, make sure you brush up on the techniques for job-hunting before you try to make the move. And above all, make sure you have secured a better position before you hand in your resignation.

#24 ... #25 ... #26

As scary as the prospect might seem, it's time to move on. Leave.

#27

What are you waiting for?

PART 5
ANSWER SHEETS

Relationships/Office Politics Test
Answer Sheet

1. a b
2. a b
3. a b
4. a b c d
5. a b c d
6. a b
7. a b c d
8. a b c d
9. a b
10. a b c
11. a b
12. a b
13. a b c
14. a b
15. a b
16. a b c
17. a b c
18. a b c d
19. a b
20. a b c d
21. a b c
22. a b c
23. a b c
24. a b c
25. a b c
26. a b
27. a b

28. a b

29. a b

30. a b

31. a b

32. a b c

33. a b

34. a b

35. a b

36. a b

37. a b

38. a b c d

39. a b c d

40. a b c d

41. a b c d

42. a b c d

43. a b c d

44. a b c

45. a b c d

46. a b c d

47. a b

48. a b

49. a b

50. a b

51. a b c d

52. a b

53. a b c d

54. a b c d

Values/Skills Test
Answer Sheet

1. a b c d e
2. a b
3. a b
4. a b
5. a b
6. a b
7. a b c
8. a b c
9. a b c
10. a b c
11. a b
12. a b
13. a b
14. a b
15. a b
16. a b
17. a b
18. a b c d e f
19. a b c d
20. a b
21. a b c d e
22. a b
23. a b
24. a b

25. a b

26. a b c d

27. a b c

28. a b c

29. a b c

30. a b

31. a b

32. a b

33. a b c

34. a b c d e

35. a b c d

36. a b

37. a b c

38. a b

39. a b

40. a b

41. a b

42. a b c

43. a b c d

44. a b c d

45. a b

46. a b

47. a b

48. a b

Company/Rewards Test
Answer Sheet

1. a b

2. a b c

3. a b

4. a b

5. a b c

6. a b c

7. a b

8. a b

9. a b

10. a b

11. a b

12. a b

13. a b

14. a b c d

15. a b c

16. a b c

17. a b

18. a b

19. a b

20. a b

21. a b c

22. a b c

23. a b

24. a b

25. a b c d e

26. a b

27. a b

28. a b

29. a b

30. a b c d

31. a b c d

32. a b c d

33. a b c d

34. a b c d

35. a b c d

36. a b c d

37. a b

38. a b

39. a b

40. a b

41. a b

42. a b c

Stress Test
Answer Sheet

1. a b c
2. a b c d
3. a b c d
4. a b c d
5. a b
6. a b c d
7. a b
8. a b
9. a b
10. a b
11. a b c d
12. a b c d
13. a b c d
14. a b c d
15. a b
16. a b c d
17. a b c d

Entrepreneurship Test
Answer Sheet

1. a b
2. a b c d
3. a b
4. a b c d
5. a b c d
6. a b
7. a b c d
8. a b c d
9. a b
10. a b
11. a b c
12. a b
13. a b
14. a b c
15. a b
16. a b
17. a b
18. a b
19. a b
20. a b
21. a b
22. a b
23. a b c d
24. a b

Job-changing Test
Answer Sheet

1. a b c d e
2. a b
3. a b
4. a b
5. a b
6. a b c
7. a b c
8. a b c d
9. a b
10. a b c d
11. a b
12. a b c d
13. a b
14. a b
15. a b
16. a b c
17. a b c
18. a b c
19. a b
20. a b c d e
21. a b c d
22. a b c
23. a b
24. a b
25. a b c
26. a b c
27. a b

ABOUT THE PEOPLE
INTERVIEWED

Paul H. Alvarez is Chairman and Chief Executive Officer of Ketchum Public Relations, the seventh-largest public relations firm in the United States. He is coauthor, with Gerlad J. Voros, of a book entitled *What Happens in Public Relations*. Paul Alvarez is one of three developers of the Ketchum Publicity Tracking Model, a computerized system for planning and evaluating publicity campaigns. He has been with Ketchum Public Relations for eighteen years.

Dr. Joyce Brothers is an author, columnist and business consultant, as well as an NBC Radio Network personality. Her six books have been translated into twenty-six languages. She is a regular columnist for *Good Housekeeping* magazine and writes a daily column that appears in newspapers throughout the world. As a consultant to the business world, Dr. Brothers creates and performs in films and leads seminars designed for corporate personnel training programs.

J. Carter Brown has been the Director of the National Gallery of Art in Washington, D.C., since 1969. He is also Chairman of the Commission of Fine Arts, Treasurer of the White House Historical Association and a Trustee of the American Academy in Rome, the John F. Kennedy Center for the Performing Arts and the National Geographic Society. Mr. Brown's honors include eleven honorary degrees, along with such distinctions as the Gold Medal of Honor, National Arts Society; the Gold Medal, National Institute of Social Sciences; and Commander, Order of Arts and Letters, France. He is the writer and director of the film *The American Vision* and a contributor to numerous journals.

Art Buchwald, columnist and author, began his career in Paris in 1948. Having enrolled at the University of Southern California under the G.I. Bill of Rights, he left without a degree and with only a $250 check he had received as a war bonus. When money ran out, he took a trial column to the European offices of the *New York Herald Tribune* and was hired to the editorial staff. Early in 1952 the editors of the *Tribune* decided to bring Mr. Buchwald's columns to readers in the United States. His columns today appear in 550 newspapers, from Oklahoma to Israel. Mr. Buchwald has more than thirty books to his credit, including *I Never Danced at the White House* and *While Reagan Slept*. He was the recipient of the Pulitzer Prize for "outstanding commentary" in 1982 and was elected to the American Academy and Institute of Arts and Letters.

Charlie Byrd has been a preeminent jazz and classical guitarist since the 1950s. In 1956 Byrd produced *Blues for Night People*, an album that marked a turning point in his professional career. He has since recorded more than fifty albums of his own and has been featured on more than two dozen others. In 1962 Byrd and saxophonist Stan Getz recorded *Jazz Samba*, and according to jazz authority

Leonard Feather, "the entire bossa nova craze in the United States may be said to have sprung directly from this album." Mr. Byrd has toured South and Central America, the Far East and Africa for the U.S. Department of State and has captured virtually every major award available to a guitarist.

Senator Alan Cranston of California is the first Democratic senator in fifty-eight years to be elected to a sixth term as his party's whip. A senator since 1969, he is chairman of the Veterans' Affairs Committee, the Subcommittee on Housing and Urban Affairs and the Subcommittee on East Asian and Pacific Affairs. Senator Cranston is the author of *The Killing of the Peace*, which was rated by the *New York Times* as one of the ten best books of 1945, and *The Big Story*.

Gary Edwards has been Executive Director of the Ethics Resource Center, in Washington, D.C., since 1981. He holds a J.D. degree from Georgetown University, as well as a master's degree from Yale. After four years in management in the for-profit sector, Mr. Edwards joined the Ethics Resource Center. On behalf of the Center he has consulted on development and implementation of standards of conduct and on ethics training for agencies like the Internal Revenue Service and the U.S. Postal Service, for the cities of Milwaukee and Chicago and for major corporations like General Dynamics and Martin Marietta.

After graduating from Barnard College, *Eileen Ford* had several jobs before beginning her modeling agency, Ford Models, Inc., with her husband, Jerry. The internationally renowned agency began with just two models and was conducted from Eileen Ford's home. She is the author of four books on modeling and beauty.

Joe Franklin is America's longest-running television host. He has conducted almost 180,000 interviews on television since his start in 1952 and has given many luminaries, including Barbra Streisand, Bill Cosby, Bette Midler and Bruce Springsteen, their first television exposure. He is host of the radio show "Joe Franklin's Memory Lane" and author of thirty-two books.

Doug Fraser began working with the United Auto Workers in 1936 and eventually became President of the entire international organization. He retired after six years in that position and took on various teaching posts. He is now Professor of Labor Studies at Wayne State University and Labor Leader in Residence at Columbia University Business School. Mr. Fraser has also served on the boards of directors of a variety of organizations, including the Full Employment Council, the NAACP, the National Urban Coalition and the National Housing Conference.

Tom Freston is President and Chief Executive Officer of MTV Networks. He has overall responsibility for the company, which operates four advertiser-supported cable television programming networks: MTV: Music Television; VH-1/Video Hits One; Nickelodeon; and Nick at Nite. Formerly President of MTV Networks Entertainment, a division of MTV Networks, Mr. Freston has made contributions that enabled MTV Networks to become one of cable television's most successful programming suppliers and one of the world's preeminent suppliers of specialized programming to demographically targeted audiences. During his tenure as President of MTV Networks Entertainment, the company launched MTV Europe and MTV Australia.

In 1979 *Mary Futrell* was a high school teacher in Alexandria, Virginia, serving on the National Education Association Board of Directors as the At-large Minority Director. She took a leave of absence from her teaching job to run for the full-time office of NEA Secretary Treasurer. In 1981 the U.S. Secretary of State appointed her to the U.S. National Commission for the United Nations Education, Scientific and Cultural Organization (UNESCO). Ms. Futrell has served as President of the NEA since 1983. In 1984 she was elected to the Executive Committee of the World Confederation of Organizations of the Teaching Profession (WCOTP).

Kevin C. Gottlieb is Staff Director of the U.S. Senate Banking Committee. Formerly he was president of a national advertising association, Senior Policy Advisor for U.S. Senator Donald Riegle and a professor in the Department of Social Science at Michigan State University. In the past he also served as, among other positions, Executive Assistant to Senator Alan Cranston, Director of the Michigan State University Comparative Public Policy Program and campaign manager for Senator Riegle's 1988 reelection bid. He has lectured throughout the country on public policy issues and holds a Ph.D. in political science.

Robert T. Gray has been Editor of *Nation's Business,* one of the country's largest business magazines, since 1982. He joined the magazine's editorial staff in 1969 after long service in the Associated Press. There he was head of the wire service's New York state capital bureau and then the AP's U.S. Senate correspondent in Washington, D.C. Mr. Gray began his journalism career as a reporter for a small newspaper in Rhode Island.

Peter D. Hart was an analyst and researcher for Louis Harris & Associates from 1964 until 1967 and became Vice-President of the company in 1971. He founded Peter D. Hart Research Associates, Inc., the next year and has become one of the leading analysts of public opinion surveys. He has been a special consultant to CBS News since 1974 and has aided such Senate leaders as Hubert Humphrey, Lloyd Bentsen, Edward Kennedy and Bill Bradley.

Judith Richards Hope is a senior partner at the Los Angeles–based firm of Paul, Hastings, Janofsky & Walker. She is the only woman on the law firm's four-member executive committee and serves as a liaison to the firm's East Coast offices. A specialist in litigation and transportation law, she served under President Ford as Associate Director of the White House Domestic Council. In the Reagan administration, she was Vice-Chairwoman of the President's Commission on Organized Crime. In 1989 she was appointed to Harvard University's highest governing board.

Larry King hosts "The Larry King Show," which airs nightly on more than 325 radio stations over the Mutual Broadcasting System, and "Larry King Live," on the Cable News Network. He also writes a weekly column, "Larry King's People," in the Monday edition of *USA Today*. He is the author of three books, most recently *Mr. King, You're Having a Heart Attack*. His broadcast career began in 1957 with a pinch-hit announcing stint on a 250-watt Miami radio station. "The Larry King Show" has won the prestigious Peabody Award, as well as the National Association of Broadcasters' 1985 award and the Jack Anderson Investigative Reporting Award. In 1986 Larry King was voted Best Radio Talk Show Host by the *Washington Journalism Review* in its annual readers' poll. "Larry King Live" is the recipient of both the 1987 and the 1988 ACE Award for excellence in cable television. Mr. King was named the International Radio and Television Society's 1989 Broadcaster of the Year. He lives in Arlington, Virginia.

Knight Kiplinger is Publisher and Editor-in-Chief of *Changing Times* magazine. He is also Vice-President for Publications of Kiplinger Washington Editors, Inc., publishers of *The Kiplinger Washington Letter, Tax Letter, Agricultural Letter, Florida Letter, California Letter, Texas Letter* and *Changing Times*. He formerly served as Washington Bureau Chief for the Ottaway Newspaper Group of Dow Jones & Co.

Gabe Mirkin, M.D., is a practicing physician as well as an author, columnist and radio host. Currently he hosts a daily radio program, "Dr. Gabe Mirkin on Health, Fitness and Nutrition," broadcasts the CBS Radio Network's daily report on fitness and nutrition and writes a syndicated column for the *New York Times*. He is the author of four books, including the national best sellers *The Sportsmedicine Book* and *Getting Thin*.

Rose Narva, widely known as "The Ultimate Innkeeper," is Director of the Jefferson Hotel in Washington, D.C. (former home base for the Reagan Cabinet). As General Manager of the Sheraton Carlton from 1975 to 1980, she oversaw its $6.9 million face-lift. From 1984 to 1985 she was General Manager of the Hay-Adams Hotel.

Jerome Navies is Director of CBS Radio Stations News Service, in Washington, D.C. In addition to covering Washington events for the stations on an individual basis, his unit produces and sells a feature package that is syndicated around the country. At KNX Radio, in Los Angeles, Mr. Navies spent ten years as a newswriter and editor and held a variety of positions in the news department.

Mike Nevard is Associate Publisher and Editorial Director of Globe Communications Corporation. He began his publishing career as a writer and editor for the British jazz weekly *Melody Maker*. From 1970 to 1978 Mr. Nevard worked on various publications owned by Rupert Murdoch, both in England and in the United States. He joined Globe Communications in 1979 and has doubled the circulation of the publishing group's three weekly tabloids, to 3,200,000.

Ike Pappas has had a distinguished career as a television and radio journalist. He spent twenty-three years at CBS news and covered the widest variety of news subjects. Today he runs Ike Pappas Network Productions in Washington, D.C., which specializes in developing news, documentary and feature programming for independent TV and radio stations, along with creating video presentations for industry, trade associations and government.

Patrick Roddy, Executive Producer of ABC's "World News This Morning" and "Good Morning America" News, began working at ABC as an engineer in 1975. From 1980 to 1982 he was a Washington producer for ABC News weekend broadcasts. He also served as Senior Producer of "This Week with David Brinkley" during the program's first year. From 1983 until May 1988 Mr. Roddy was Senior Producer of "World News This Morning" and "Good Morning America" News.

Stephen I. Schlossberg was General Counsel and Director of Government Affairs of the United Automobile Workers of America (U.A.W.) for nearly twenty years. He is now Director of the Washington branch of the International Labor Office and Special Advisor to the Director-General of the I.L.O. Mr. Schlossberg was appointed by President Reagan to the President's Commission on Industrial Competitiveness and by President Carter to the President's Advisory Board on Ambassadorial Appointments. He is a former adjunct professor of law at Georgetown University Law Center.

After a short but very successful career as an advertising executive, *Paul Sorvino* turned back to the acting profession. He has appeared in more than twenty-five films, among them *Reds, Bloodbrothers* and *A Touch of Class.* On stage he won the New York Drama Critics Circle Award and a Tony nomination for best actor, in *That Championship Season.* He has recorded two Broadway show albums and is the author of the best seller *How to Become a Former Asthmatic.* Mr. Sorvino is now pursuing an operatic career.

Paul Steinle, President and Chief Executive Officer of United Press International, was previously President and Chief Executive Officer of Financial News Network. He has over twenty years of experience in broadcast journalism and electronic publishing. He coauthored *Commune: Life in Rural China* and received the Overseas Press Club citation for excellence in radio reporting in Vietnam in 1972.

Currently President and Chief Operating Officer of Loews Corporation, *Preston Robert Tisch* served as United States Postmaster General from 1986 to 1988. He also serves as Chairman Emeritus of the New York Convention and Visitors Bureau, a Trustee of New York University, Chairman of the Tisch School of the Arts and a Director of City Meals-on-Wheels. Preston Tisch is also credited with coining the phrase "power breakfast."

Jack Valenti has been President and Chief Executive Officer of the Motion Picture Association of America, Inc., since 1966. In this capacity he has served as the leader of the film production and distribution industry in this country and in more than one hundred countries where American films are exhibited. After getting an M.B.A. from Harvard University, he founded an advertising and political consulting agency in Houston. From 1963 to 1966 he was Special Assistant to President Lyndon Johnson. He is the author of three books and numerous magazine articles.

Caspar Willard Weinberger served as Secretary of Defense from 1981 until his resignation in 1987. Previously he had been director of several companies—PepsiCo, Inc., Quaker Oats Co., and the Bechtel Group. Mr. Weinberger was also a member of the Trilateral Commission, a member of the Board of Trustees of St. Luke's Hospital in San Francisco and Chairman of the hospital's National Trustees. In addition, he was Chairman of the National Trustees of the National Symphony Orchestra in Washington, D.C. In January 1989 Mr. Weinberger became Publisher of *Forbes* magazine.

After military service in World War II, *Eddie R. White* became a songwriter for such singers as Frank Sinatra, Tony Bennett, Patti Page, Eddie Fisher and Cab Calloway. He later produced the Broadway play *The Family Way,* as well as many concerts in the United States and Japan. From 1960 to 1969 Mr. White worked for Yamaha in Japan, eventually becoming Vice-President. As an actor, he has appeared in *The Killer Elite, Manhattan,* and *Short Eyes,* among others. He is also the author of *Yesterday's Cake.*

George F. Will, columnist and author, came to Washington, D.C., as a congressional aide to Colorado senator Gordon Allott. In 1972 he became the Washington editor of *The National Review.* His newspaper column has been syndicated since 1974 and now appears in more than 460 newspapers. In 1977 he won the Pulitzer Prize for commentary, for these columns. He has published three collections of his columns, as well as a work of political philosophy. He is also a television news analyst for the ABC–Capital Cities network. In 1981 he became a founding member of the panel of ABC's "This Week with David Brinkley."

Bob Woodward, now the Assistant Managing Editor of the investigative unit at the *Washington Post,* began at the *Post* in 1971. He teamed with Carl Bernstein to investigate the break-in at the Democratic Headquarters in the Watergate office building. The *Post* was awarded the Pulitzer Prize in 1973 for its reporting of the Watergate scandals. Woodward and Bernstein coauthored two best-selling books, *All the President's Men* and *The Final Days.* Mr. Woodward also wrote *Wired* and *VEIL: The Secret Wars of the CIA 1981–1987.*

V. Orville Wright is Vice-Chairman and Member of the Office of Chief Executive of MCI Communications Corporation. He was both a Marketing Director and Director of Systems and Technology for IBM, Vice-President of Business Development for Xerox Corporation, Vice-President of Marketing for Amdahl

Corporation and President of RCA's Computer Systems Development division. He joined MCI in 1975.

Duke Zeibert, owner of the popular Washington, D.C., restaurant that bears his name, worked as a general manager of many restaurants around the United States in the 1940s. In 1950 he opened Duke Zeibert's and oversaw its daily operations for over thirty years. In 1983 he arranged for the restaurant to be torn down and rebuilt as part of the Washington Square complex.

Acknowledgments

With special thanks to:

The brilliant mind of agent and friend Reid Boates, who sold this book and gave us excellent editorial advice. It was fun putting your brainstorm to work in our style.

Our agent and friend of long standing, Julian Bach, a legend in his own right.

We are blessed with you both.

The keen eye and gift for choosing books that live on forever of Harper & Row Associate Publisher, Director of Reference Publishing, Carol Cohen.

William Shinker, Publisher, Harper & Row Trade Division, for his faith in *Stay or Leave.*

Our software agent, Carolyn Kuhn, for suggesting interviews for this book.

You, the well known who generously gave your time to tell your story. And to your gatekeepers, for without their help many of your stories would not have been told.

Roxanne Lewis for painstakingly typing and retyping the manuscript.

Friend John Lyons, award-winning creative advertising director and author of *Guts,* for sharing your personal stylebook of writing with Sister Bernadine and me.

And to all those who are good at what they do, but not necessarily happy on the job. Your personal insights and input were invaluable.

Fondest memories during the *Stay or Leave* project:

Scott L. Gale for sharing his pad during the eight-month commute from Manhattan to Washington.

Friends Liz Schrayer, David Gillete, Sarah Ehrman, Lisa Landau, Nathaniel Lack, Amy Cooper, Matt Yelcich, Carman Jimasen and Audry Prescott . . . smiling faces, friendly chats and people who care.

Attorney John Carey, for your patience, understanding and time spent teaching the art of negotiation.

Legal eagle Bob Pomerenk: You truly fill your career niche with honor.

The times invited to dine in splendor at the Jefferson Hotel in Washington, D.C., by its gracious hostess and managing director, Rose Narva.

Mel Krupin's. The Prime Rib. The German Deli (Cafe Mozart). Ramparts. El Chalan.

1744 and 619.